Helping Children Learn
Basic
Math
Skills

Congratulations on your purchase of some of the finest teaching materials in the world.

Entire contents of compiled version copyright ©1994
by EVAN-MOOR CORP.
18 Lower Ragsdale Drive, Monterey, CA 93940-5746

Author: Jo Ellen Moore
Illustrator: Joy Evans
Editor: Michelle Tapola

Original editions:
Beginning Multiplication, © 1988 by Evan-Moor Corp.
Telling Time - Level C, © 1986 by Evan-Moor Corp.
Practice Money Skills - Level C, © 1985 by Evan-Moor Corp.
Problem Solving - Level B, © 1985 by Evan-Moor Corp.
Problem Solving - Level C, © 1985 by Evan-Moor Corp.
Math Mysteries, © 1986 by Evan-Moor Corp.
Practice Addition and Subtraction, © 1988 by Evan-Moor Corp.
Puzzles and Patterns, © 1986 by Evan-Moor Corp.
Math Packs - Multiplication & Division, © 1985 by Evan-Moor Corp.
Division Basic Facts, © 1994 by Evan-Moor Corp.

Evan-Moor
HELPING CHILDREN LEARN

Addition
and
Subtraction

These pages provide students with practice in addition and subtraction involving:

- *multi-digit numbers*

- *regrouping to find the sum or difference*

Answer Key

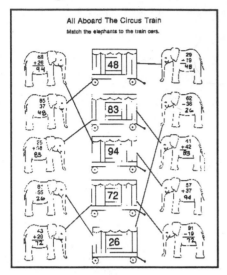

Page 6:

Page 7:

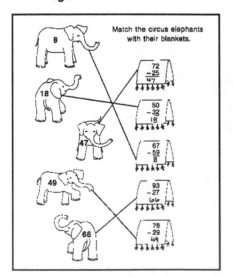

Page 8:

They can't go in
the swimming pool
without them.

Page 9:

See picture

Page 10:

Because the
corn has ears!

Page 11:

$10.75 $ 9.88 $34.47 $55.34
$68.49 $15.98 $67.59 $47.77
$ 2.59 $ 4.00 $15.36 $23.28

Page 12:

He sits on an acorn and
waits for it to grow.

Page 13:

418   335   374   423   264
371   423   235   229   223
3628   5161   1303   2210   2533

Bonus:

335   426   378   689   379

Super Bonus:

3,239,484   7,765,433

Page 14:

955
810   991
7,198   9,219   6,340
10,017   5,157   9,825   86,341

Super Bonus:

93,591   52,221   103,340   1,357,688

Basic Math Skills 3

All Aboard the Circus Train

Match the elephants to the train cars.

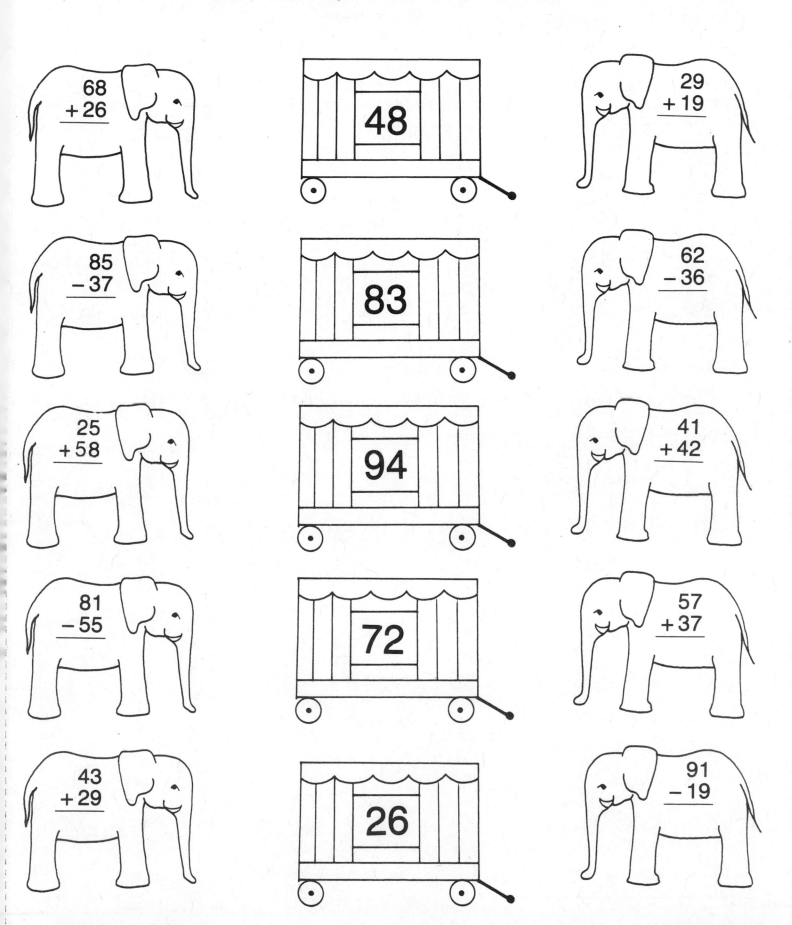

68
+ 26

85
− 37

25
+ 58

81
− 55

43
+ 29

48

83

94

72

26

29
+ 19

62
− 36

41
+ 42

57
+ 37

91
− 19

Basic Math Skills 3

Color the 18s red to find the
elephant that ate the peanuts.

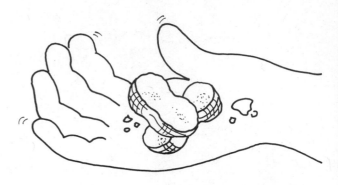

44 −26	21 −5	63 −49	98 −79	76 −38	97 −24
72 −39	70 −52	53 −35	85 −65	47 −27	23 −16
82 −67	32 −26	35 −19	97 −79	46 −27	60 −46
40 −29	51 −27	38 −19	50 −25	32 −14	81 −63
64 −37	58 −36	78 −59	25 −17	84 −62	65 −47

Basic Math Skills 3

8

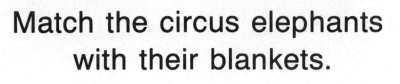

Match the circus elephants with their blankets.

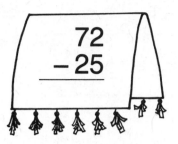

$$\begin{array}{r} 72 \\ -25 \\ \hline \end{array}$$

18

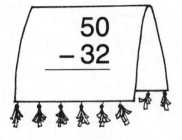

$$\begin{array}{r} 50 \\ -32 \\ \hline \end{array}$$

47

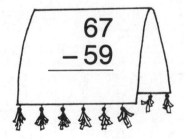

$$\begin{array}{r} 67 \\ -59 \\ \hline \end{array}$$

49

$$\begin{array}{r} 93 \\ -27 \\ \hline \end{array}$$

66

$$\begin{array}{r} 78 \\ -29 \\ \hline \end{array}$$

Basic Math Skills 3

Why do elephants have trunks?

45-c   68-y   87-w
48-u   70-p   91-e
54-a   75-h   93-t
56-n   77-g   96-s
61-l   80-m
62-i   84- o

37	59	63	19
+ 56	+ 16	+ 28	+ 49

26	17	38	48
+ 19	+ 37	+ 18	+ 45

28	29
+ 49	+ 55

33	27
+ 29	+ 29

28	38	49
+ 65	+ 37	+ 42

67	39	26	53	46	14	49	39
+ 29	+ 48	+ 36	+ 27	+ 34	+ 48	+ 7	+ 38

46	66	37	35
+ 24	+ 18	+ 47	+ 26

18	45	76	47	48	19	65
+ 69	+ 17	+ 17	+ 28	+ 36	+ 29	+ 28

54	26	27	65
+ 39	+ 49	+ 64	+ 15

       Basic Math Skills 3

Patchwork Elephant

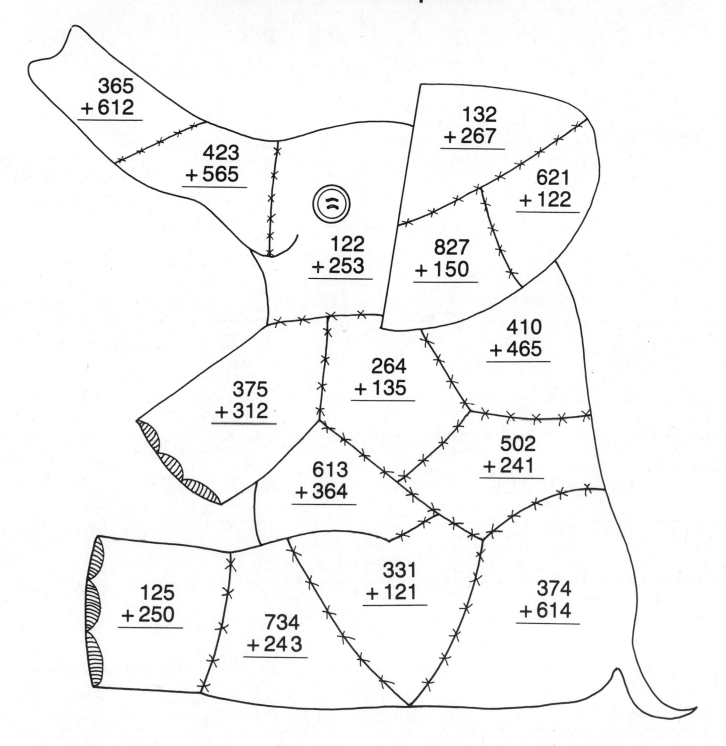

375 — green
399 — yellow stripes
452 — yellow
687 — yellow dots

743 — green dots
875 — red dots
977 — red
988 — green stripes

Basic Math Skills 3

Why won't elephants tell secrets in a cornfield?

25-e	42-r	77-h
28-t	53-a	85-c
37-o	61-b	90-s
39-n		96-u

24 +37	52 −27	38 +47	82 −29	48 +48	62 +28	13 +12

80 −52	38 +39	94 −69

——— —— —— —— —— —— ——   —— —— ——

59 +26	72 −35	26 +16	65 −26

95 −18	70 −17	55 +35

—— —— —— ——   —— —— ——

71 −46	27 +26	81 −39	46 +44

—— —— —— —— —— !

Basic Math Skills 3

Elephants For Sale

How much will we cost?

$4.65 + 6.10	$5.23 + 4.65	$12.25 + 22.22	$41.04 + 14.30

$41.04 22.22 + 5.23	$4.65 5.23 + 6.10	$12.25 14.30 + 41.04	$22.22 13.30 + 12.25

How much more do we cost?

$8.69 − 6.10	$8.69 − 4.69	$37.58 − 22.22	$37.58 − 14.30

11

Basic Math Skills 3

How does an elephant get up in a tree?

111-s
130-t
175-h
212-o
297-f
303-r
321-c

425-i
482-e
536-n
555-d
600-g
674-a
747-w

586	589
− 411	− 107

437	935	353	624
− 326	− 510	− 223	− 513

496	767
− 284	− 231

977	999
− 303	− 463

786	477	868	943	688
− 112	− 156	− 656	− 640	− 152

796	676	777
− 122	− 140	− 222

998	889	589	781	581
− 251	− 215	− 164	− 651	− 470

798	539	528
− 501	− 327	− 225

657	476
− 232	− 346

592	925
− 462	− 713

773	795	794	869
− 173	− 492	− 582	− 122

12   Basic Math Skills 3

```
 735      960      806      951      428
-317     -625     -432     -528     -164
```

```
 651      742      383      294      615
-280     -319     -148     - 65     -392
```

```
 4982     7659     2931     7039     5168
-1354    -2498    -1628    -4829    -2635
```

Bonus!

```
 600      813      526      987      765
-265     -387     -148     -298     -386
```

Super Bonus!!

```
  5936842        9000000
 -2697358       -1234567
```

Basic Math Skills 3

Can you find the answers before this hungry elephant eats all of the hay?

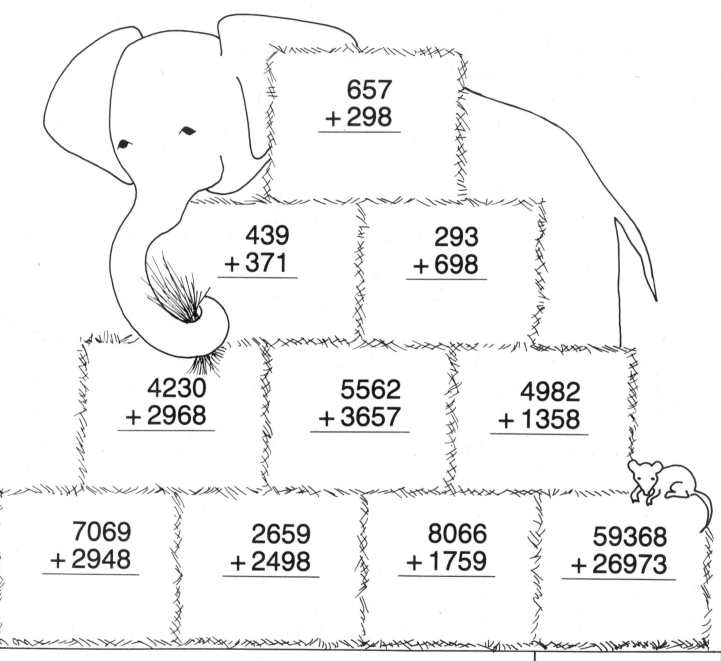

$$657 + 298$$

$$439 + 371$$

$$293 + 698$$

$$4230 + 2968$$

$$5562 + 3657$$

$$4982 + 1358$$

$$7069 + 2948$$

$$2659 + 2498$$

$$8066 + 1759$$

$$59368 + 26973$$

Super Bonus

$$65983 + 27608$$

$$12345 + 39876$$

$$86351 + 16989$$

$$999999 + 357689$$

Basic Math Skills 3

Beginning Multiplication
Basic Facts through 9

These pages were designed to motivate children to practice the basic multiplication facts.

- *basic facts 1- 9*

- *one-digit times two-digit numbers*

- *one-digit times three-digit numbers*

Basic Math Skills 3

Answer Key

Page 18:
see picture
4 1 0 0 6 12
2 8 3 10 4 16
12 2 7 18 8 14

Page 19:

0	0	0	0
0	1	2	3
0	2	4	6
0	3	6	9
0	4	8	12
0	5	10	15
0	6	12	18
0	7	14	21
0	8	16	24
0	9	18	27

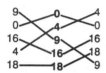

Page 20:

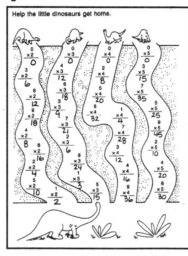

Page 21:
see picture

Page 22:
7 0 10 16 1 4
3 8 0 6 28 9
21 15 32 12 27 20
12 24 24 18 36 4

Page 23:
see picture

Page 24:
Triceratops
Pteranodon

Page 25:

Page 26:
0 8 4 4 5 0 6 2
3 10 9 6 15 20 16 8
0 12 15 9 10 12 8 18
20 12 21 24 25 45 7 32
30 14 24 6 20 36 0 40
16 28 16 27 35 0 4 18

Page 27:

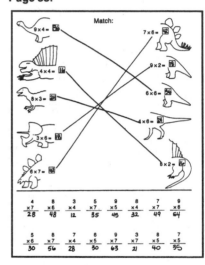

Page 28:
see picture
Multiply 0 thru 9 by 6s
0 6 12 18 24 30 36 42 48 54
24 20 0 20 10 12 36 30
12 6 28 40 18 32 36 54
42 15 30 15 48 45 24 35

Page 29:
see picture
Multiply 0 thru 9 by 7s
0 7 14 21 28 35 42 49 56 63
0 0 14 35 7 54 21 28
56 14 18 63 28 54 28 35
42 54 21 42 30 14 48 63

Page 30:

0	12	63	7
14	28	18	35
	24	54	48
	6	30	45
	36	21	25
	49	42	56
			42

Page 31:
see picture

Page 32:
see picture

Page 33:

(Match diagram)

4	6	3	5	9	8	7	8
×7	×6	×4	×7	×5	×4	×7	×8
28	48	12	35	45	32	49	64

5	8	7	6	9	3	8	7
×6	×7	×4	×5	×7	×7	×5	×5
30	56	28	30	63	21	40	35

Page 34:
Her pink ones were
in the wash!

Page 35:
see picture
Multiply 0 thru 9 by 8s
0 8 16 24 32 40 48 56 64 72
0 12 8 28 24 25 24 40
16 35 48 18 56 56 14 32
27 64 42 20 72 9 30 63

Page 36:
6 16 0 12 0 8 14 7
18 25 36 9 42 18 64 21
42 24 10 54 28 16 48 49
56 18 30 6 32 18 4 21
56 1 24 0 36 21 40 35
35 32 10 12 72 48 15 63

Basic Math Skills 3

(Answer key continued)

Page 37:

24 35 56 24 10 72 16 15
36 64 21 40 0 35 36 56
32 42 15 63 14 32 30 20
30 21 48 18 42 18 25 54
18 45 10 28 21 48 8 49

Page 38:

Elasmosaurus
Stegosaurus

Page 39:

This could be the start
of something big!

Page 40:

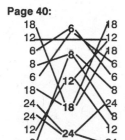

Page 41:

see picture

Page 42:

0	7	24
0	7	24
28	72	54
28	72	54
40	63	48
40	63	48
45	21	36
45	21	36
56	27	42
56	27	42
18	35	32
18	35	32
81	64	49

Page 43:

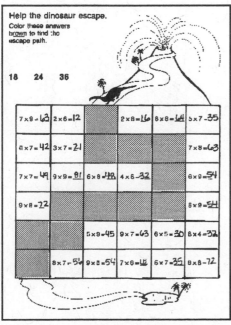

Page 44:

see picture
Multiply 0 thru 9 by 9s

16 27 0 56 9 36 40 45
18 0 8 45 24 45 81 48
72 32 54 56 72 63 64 54

Page 45:

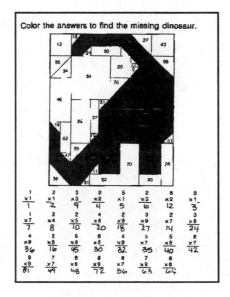

Page 46:

see picture

Page 47:

Pteranodon - 155
Elasmosaurus - 448
Ichthyosaurus - 630
Tylosaurus - 427
Geosaurus - 448

Page 48:

128 249
288 400 97 864
255 78 260 114 744
216 405 602 375 972

Bonus:

695 2120 4501 5238 3804

Page 49:

(timed test)
0 0 1 4 15 30
6 0 5 18 12 20
27 6 0 4 9 12
0 14 8 0 2 24
10 3 21 25 18 16

Page 50:

(timed test)
0 7 36 12 21 32
36 35 32 0 54 24
49 28 24 8 18 18
45 16 36 18 9 14
21 0 30 14 40 18

Basic Math Skills 3

Start at 0.

The Pteranodon was a flying dinosaur.
It had long wings and a crest on its head.

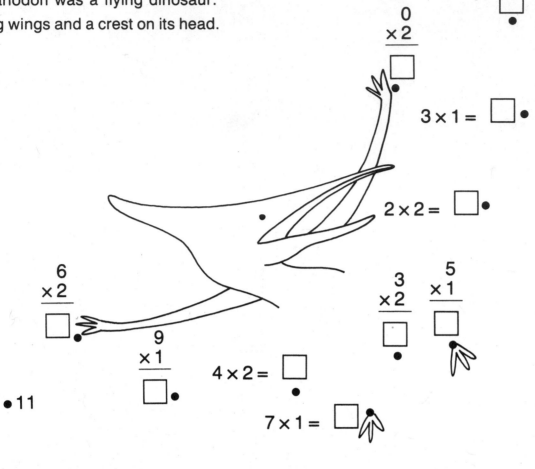

$$\begin{array}{r} 1 \\ \times 1 \\ \hline \square \end{array}$$

$$\begin{array}{r} 1 \\ \times 2 \\ \hline \square \end{array}$$

$$\begin{array}{r} 0 \\ \times 2 \\ \hline \square \end{array}$$

$3 \times 1 = \square$

$2 \times 2 = \square$

$$\begin{array}{r} 6 \\ \times 2 \\ \hline \square \end{array}$$

$$\begin{array}{r} 3 \\ \times 2 \\ \hline \square \end{array}$$

$$\begin{array}{r} 5 \\ \times 1 \\ \hline \square \end{array}$$

$$\begin{array}{r} 9 \\ \times 1 \\ \hline \square \end{array}$$

$4 \times 2 = \square$

•11

$$\begin{array}{r} 5 \\ \times 2 \\ \hline \square \end{array}$$

$7 \times 1 = \square$

$$\begin{array}{r} 2 \\ \times 2 \\ \hline \end{array} \qquad \begin{array}{r} 1 \\ \times 1 \\ \hline \end{array} \qquad \begin{array}{r} 0 \\ \times 1 \\ \hline \end{array} \qquad \begin{array}{r} 0 \\ \times 2 \\ \hline \end{array} \qquad \begin{array}{r} 3 \\ \times 2 \\ \hline \end{array} \qquad \begin{array}{r} 6 \\ \times 2 \\ \hline \end{array}$$

$$\begin{array}{r} 2 \\ \times 1 \\ \hline \end{array} \qquad \begin{array}{r} 4 \\ \times 2 \\ \hline \end{array} \qquad \begin{array}{r} 3 \\ \times 1 \\ \hline \end{array} \qquad \begin{array}{r} 5 \\ \times 2 \\ \hline \end{array} \qquad \begin{array}{r} 4 \\ \times 1 \\ \hline \end{array} \qquad \begin{array}{r} 8 \\ \times 2 \\ \hline \end{array}$$

$$\begin{array}{r} 6 \\ \times 2 \\ \hline \end{array} \qquad \begin{array}{r} 1 \\ \times 2 \\ \hline \end{array} \qquad \begin{array}{r} 7 \\ \times 1 \\ \hline \end{array} \qquad \begin{array}{r} 9 \\ \times 2 \\ \hline \end{array} \qquad \begin{array}{r} 8 \\ \times 1 \\ \hline \end{array} \qquad \begin{array}{r} 7 \\ \times 2 \\ \hline \end{array}$$

Basic Math Skills 3

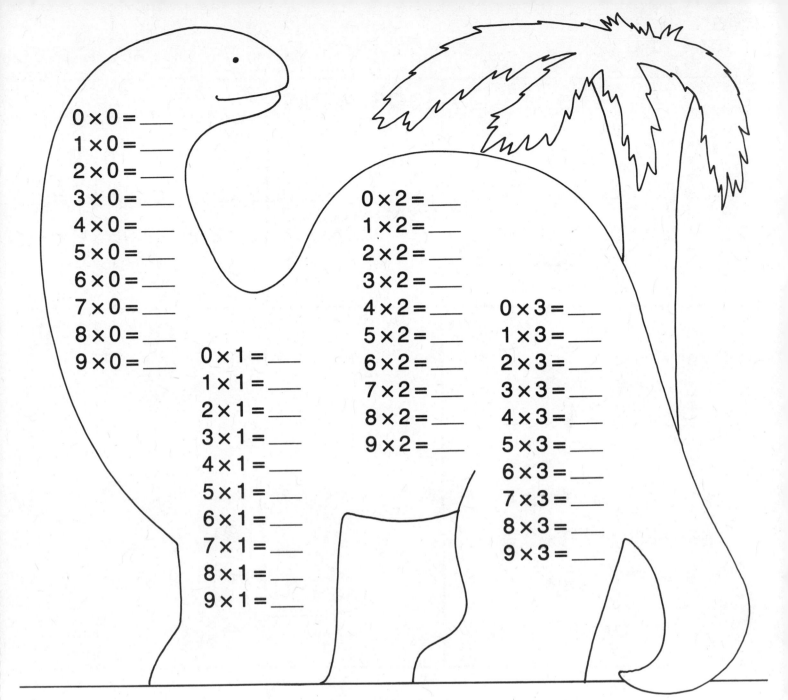

0 × 0 = ___
1 × 0 = ___
2 × 0 = ___
3 × 0 = ___
4 × 0 = ___
5 × 0 = ___
6 × 0 = ___
7 × 0 = ___
8 × 0 = ___
9 × 0 = ___

0 × 1 = ___
1 × 1 = ___
2 × 1 = ___
3 × 1 = ___
4 × 1 = ___
5 × 1 = ___
6 × 1 = ___
7 × 1 = ___
8 × 1 = ___
9 × 1 = ___

0 × 2 = ___
1 × 2 = ___
2 × 2 = ___
3 × 2 = ___
4 × 2 = ___
5 × 2 = ___
6 × 2 = ___
7 × 2 = ___
8 × 2 = ___
9 × 2 = ___

0 × 3 = ___
1 × 3 = ___
2 × 3 = ___
3 × 3 = ___
4 × 3 = ___
5 × 3 = ___
6 × 3 = ___
7 × 3 = ___
8 × 3 = ___
9 × 3 = ___

Match:

3 × 3 =	**0**	1 × 4 =
0 × 3 =	**4**	9 × 0 =
8 × 2 =	**9**	4 × 4 =
2 × 2 =	**16**	9 × 2 =
6 × 3 =	**18**	9 × 1 =

Basic Math Skills 3

Start at 0.

Geosaurus

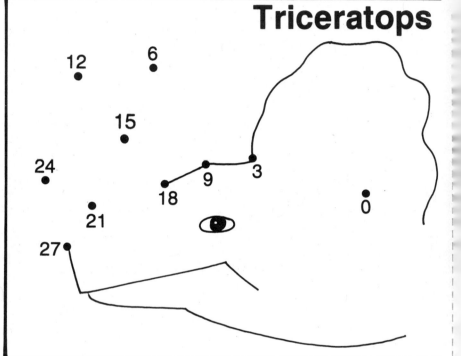

0 × 2 = ___   5 × 2 = ___

1 × 2 = ___   6 × 2 = ___

2 × 2 = ___   7 × 2 = ___

3 × 2 = ___   8 × 2 = ___

4 × 2 = ___   9 × 2 = ___

0 × 3 = ___   5 × 3 = ___

1 × 3 = ___   6 × 3 = ___

2 × 3 = ___   7 × 3 = ___

3 × 3 = ___   8 × 3 = ___

4 × 3 = ___   9 × 3 = ___

Triceratops

$$\begin{array}{cccccc}
2 & 3 & 2 & 3 & 0 & 6 \\
\times 3 & \times 2 & \times 2 & \times 3 & \times 3 & \times 3 \\
\hline
\end{array}$$

$$\begin{array}{cccccc}
1 & 4 & 7 & 5 & 8 & 7 \\
\times 3 & \times 2 & \times 3 & \times 2 & \times 3 & \times 2 \\
\hline
\end{array}$$

$$\begin{array}{cccccc}
8 & 4 & 9 & 5 & 6 & 9 \\
\times 2 & \times 3 & \times 2 & \times 3 & \times 2 & \times 3 \\
\hline
\end{array}$$

Cut and paste to find the dinosaur.

2 × 3 = ☐	4 × 4 = ☐
7 × 4 = ☐	6 × 3 = ☐
9 × 3 = ☐	5 × 4 = ☐
5 × 3 = ☐	9 × 4 = ☐
8 × 4 = ☐	7 × 3 = ☐
4 × 3 = ☐	6 × 4 = ☐

18	20
15	24
16	32
21	6
27	36
28	12

Basic Math Skills 3

A Dimetrodon was about twelve feet long.
It had a huge sail on its back.
The Dimetrodon was a meat eater.

7	0	5	8	1	2
×1	×1	×2	×2	×1	×2

1	2	0	2	7	3
×3	×4	×3	×3	×4	×3

7	5	8	3	9	5
×3	×3	×4	×4	×3	×4

4	6	8	6	9	1
×3	×4	×3	×3	×4	×4

Cut and paste to find the hidden dinosaur.

4 ×4	7 ×5	2 ×5	5 ×4	9 ×5	3 ×4
1 ×5	7 ×4	3 ×5	2 ×4	6 ×5	8 ×4
1 ×4	5 ×5	9 ×4	8 ×5	0 ×4	6 ×4

23

Basic Math Skills 3

Who Am I?

0-t   12-a   20-p
4-s   15-e   24-n
6-o   16-r   28-g
9-d   18-u   32-c
10-i   36-y

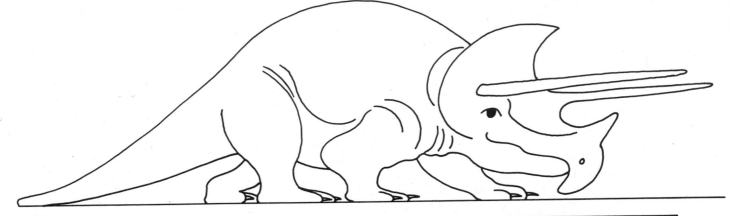

4×0	4×4	5×2	8×4	3×5	8×2	4×3	3×0	1×6	5×4	1×4

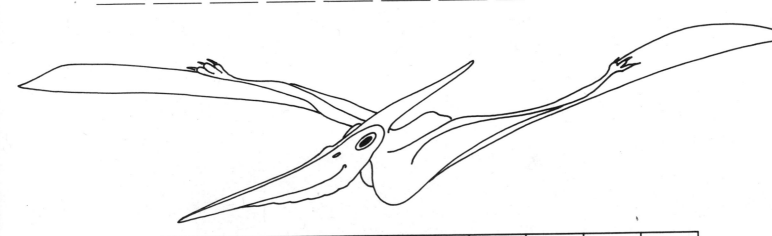

4×5	5×0	5×3	4×4	6×2	6×4	6×1	9×1	1×6	8×3

Basic Math Skills 3

0 × 0 = ___   0 × 1 = ___   0 × 2 = ___
1 × 0 = ___   1 × 1 = ___   1 × 2 = ___
2 × 0 = ___   2 × 1 = ___   2 × 2 = ___
3 × 0 = ___   3 × 1 = ___   3 × 2 = ___
4 × 0 = ___   4 × 1 = ___   4 × 2 = ___
5 × 0 = ___   5 × 1 = ___   5 × 2 = ___
6 × 0 = ___   6 × 1 = ___   6 × 2 = ___
7 × 0 = ___   7 × 1 = ___   7 × 2 = ___
8 × 0 = ___   8 × 1 = ___   8 × 2 = ___
9 × 0 = ___   9 × 1 = ___   9 × 2 = ___

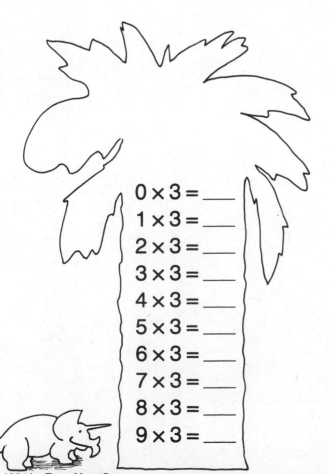

0 × 3 = ___
1 × 3 = ___
2 × 3 = ___
3 × 3 = ___
4 × 3 = ___
5 × 3 = ___
6 × 3 = ___
7 × 3 = ___
8 × 3 = ___
9 × 3 = ___

0 × 4 = ___   0 × 5 = ___
1 × 4 = ___   1 × 5 = ___
2 × 4 = ___   2 × 5 = ___
3 × 4 = ___   3 × 5 = ___
4 × 4 = ___   4 × 5 = ___
5 × 4 = ___   5 × 5 = ___
6 × 4 = ___   6 × 5 = ___
7 × 4 = ___   7 × 5 = ___
8 × 4 = ___   8 × 5 = ___
9 × 4 = ___   9 × 5 = ___

Basic Math Skills 3

Dinosaur Relay

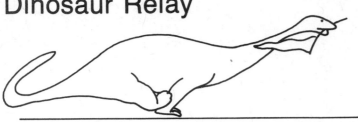

0 ×5	4 ×2	1 ×4	2 ×2	5 ×1	4 ×0	3 ×2	1 ×2
1 ×3	5 ×2	3 ×3	3 ×2	5 ×3	4 ×5	4 ×4	4 ×2
0 ×2	4 ×3	3 ×5	9 ×1	5 ×2	3 ×4	8 ×1	6 ×3
5 ×4	6 ×2	7 ×3	6 ×4	5 ×5	9 ×5	7 ×1	8 ×4
6 ×5	7 ×2	8 ×3	6 ×1	4 ×5	9 ×4	6 ×0	8 ×5
8 ×2	7 ×4	8 ×2	9 ×3	7 ×5	0 ×7	4 ×1	9 ×2

Basic Math Skills 3

Help the little dinosaurs get home.

0 ×2	0 ×3	0 ×4	0 ×5
3 ×2	4 ×3	2 ×4	3 ×5
6 ×2	6 ×3	5 ×4	7 ×5
9 ×2	3 ×3	8 ×4	5 ×5
4 ×2	7 ×3	1 ×4	9 ×5
8 ×2	2 ×3	7 ×4	2 ×5
2 ×2	8 ×3	3 ×4	4 ×5
5 ×2	1 ×3	4 ×4	6 ×5
1 ×2	5 ×3	9 ×4	

Basic Math Skills 3

Lambeosaurus

Start at 0.

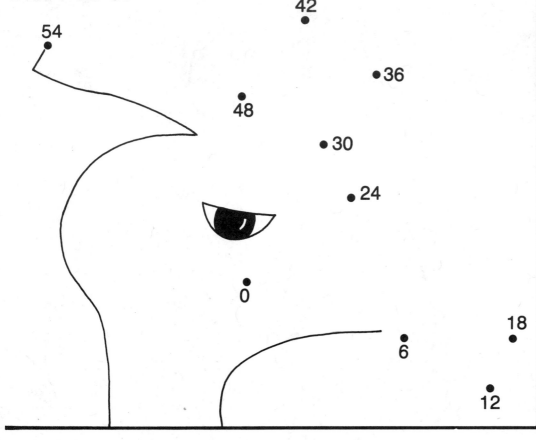

0 × 6 = _____
1 × 6 = _____
2 × 6 = _____
3 × 6 = _____
4 × 6 = _____
5 × 6 = _____
6 × 6 = _____
7 × 6 = _____
8 × 6 = _____
9 × 6 = _____

4 ×6	5 ×4	0 ×6	4 ×5	2 ×5	2 ×6	9 ×4	6 ×5
3 ×4	1 ×6	7 ×4	8 ×5	3 ×6	8 ×4	6 ×6	9 ×6
7 ×6	3 ×5	5 ×6	3 ×5	8 ×6	9 ×5	6 ×4	7 ×5

Basic Math Skills 3

Protoceratops

Start at 0.

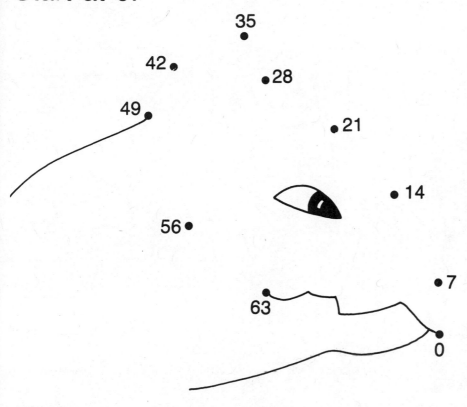

$$0 \times 7 = \underline{\hspace{2em}}$$
$$1 \times 7 = \underline{\hspace{2em}}$$
$$2 \times 7 = \underline{\hspace{2em}}$$
$$3 \times 7 = \underline{\hspace{2em}}$$
$$4 \times 7 = \underline{\hspace{2em}}$$
$$5 \times 7 = \underline{\hspace{2em}}$$
$$6 \times 7 = \underline{\hspace{2em}}$$
$$7 \times 7 = \underline{\hspace{2em}}$$
$$8 \times 7 = \underline{\hspace{2em}}$$
$$9 \times 7 = \underline{\hspace{2em}}$$

0	0	2	7	1	9	3	4
×6	×7	×7	×5	×7	×6	×7	×7

8	2	6	9	4	9	7	5
×7	×7	×3	×7	×7	×6	×4	×7

6	9	3	7	6	7	8	9
×7	×6	×7	×6	×5	×2	×6	×7

Basic Math Skills 3

The Stegosaurus was eighteen feet long and weighed two or three tons. It had bony plates along its back and spikes on its tail.

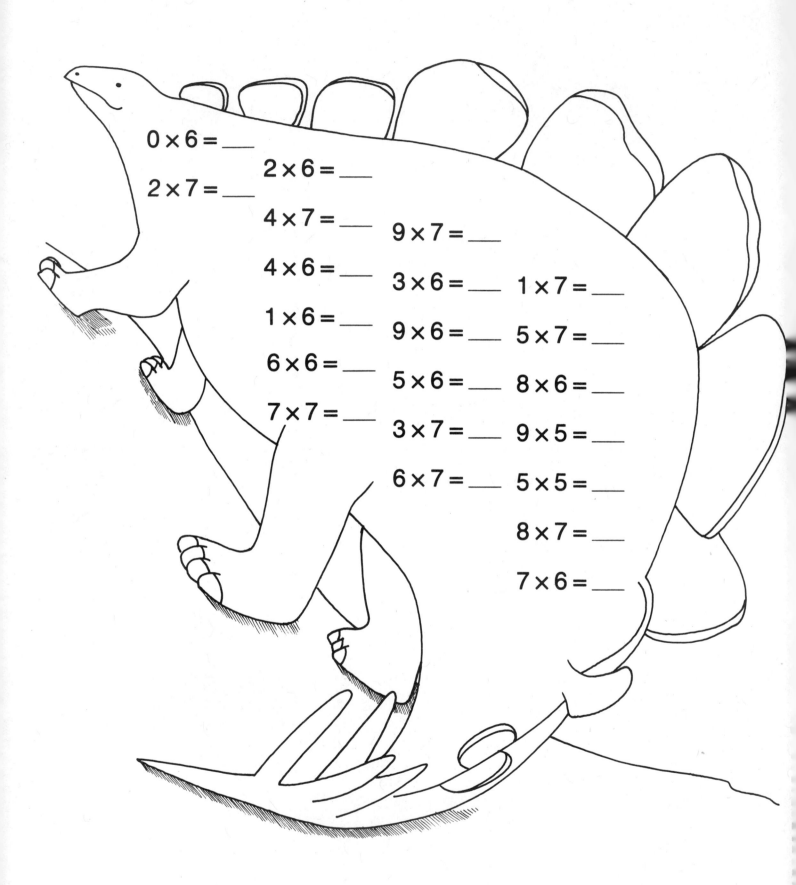

$0 \times 6 =$ __

$2 \times 6 =$ __

$2 \times 7 =$ __

$4 \times 7 =$ __

$9 \times 7 =$ __

$4 \times 6 =$ __

$3 \times 6 =$ __ $1 \times 7 =$ __

$1 \times 6 =$ __

$9 \times 6 =$ __ $5 \times 7 =$ __

$6 \times 6 =$ __

$5 \times 6 =$ __ $8 \times 6 =$ __

$7 \times 7 =$ __

$3 \times 7 =$ __ $9 \times 5 =$ __

$6 \times 7 =$ __ $5 \times 5 =$ __

$8 \times 7 =$ __

$7 \times 6 =$ __

Basic Math Skills 3

Start at 1.

The Brontosaurus (Apatosaurus) was seventy-five feet long and weighed twenty tons. It was a plant eater. Sometimes it traveled with a herd.

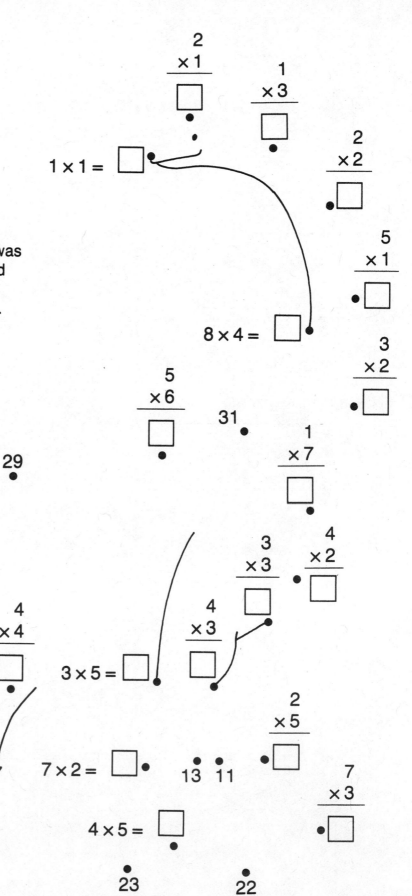

$1 \times 1 =$ ☐

$8 \times 4 =$ ☐

$\begin{array}{r} 2 \\ \times 1 \\ \hline \end{array}$ ☐

$\begin{array}{r} 1 \\ \times 3 \\ \hline \end{array}$ ☐

$\begin{array}{r} 2 \\ \times 2 \\ \hline \end{array}$ ☐

$\begin{array}{r} 5 \\ \times 1 \\ \hline \end{array}$ ☐

$\begin{array}{r} 3 \\ \times 2 \\ \hline \end{array}$ ☐

$\begin{array}{r} 5 \\ \times 6 \\ \hline \end{array}$ ☐

31

$\begin{array}{r} 1 \\ \times 7 \\ \hline \end{array}$ ☐

29

$\begin{array}{r} 4 \\ \times 7 \\ \hline \end{array}$ ☐

$9 \times 3 =$ ☐

26

$\begin{array}{r} 6 \\ \times 3 \\ \hline \end{array}$ ☐

$5 \times 5 =$ ☐

$4 \times 6 =$ ☐

$\begin{array}{r} 4 \\ \times 4 \\ \hline \end{array}$ ☐

17

19

$3 \times 5 =$ ☐

$7 \times 2 =$ ☐

$\begin{array}{r} 4 \\ \times 3 \\ \hline \end{array}$ ☐

$\begin{array}{r} 3 \\ \times 3 \\ \hline \end{array}$ ☐

$\begin{array}{r} 4 \\ \times 2 \\ \hline \end{array}$ ☐

13   11

$\begin{array}{r} 2 \\ \times 5 \\ \hline \end{array}$ ☐

$4 \times 5 =$ ☐

$\begin{array}{r} 7 \\ \times 3 \\ \hline \end{array}$ ☐

23   22

Basic Math Skills 3

Cut and paste to find the hidden dinosaur.

0 ×7	3 ×6	1 ×6	4 ×7	6 ×6	7 ×7
1 ×7	5 ×7	4 ×6	8 ×7	2 ×6	5 ×6
8 ×6	9 ×7	2 ×7	3 ×7	9 ×6	6 ×7

32

Basic Math Skills 3

Match:

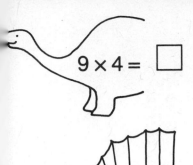

$9 \times 4 = \square$

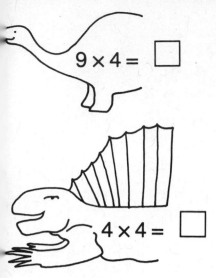

$4 \times 4 = \square$

$8 \times 3 = \square$

$3 \times 6 = \square$

$6 \times 7 = \square$

$7 \times 6 = \square$

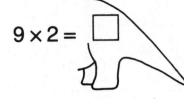

$9 \times 2 = \square$

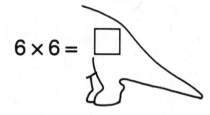

$6 \times 6 = \square$

$4 \times 6 = \square$

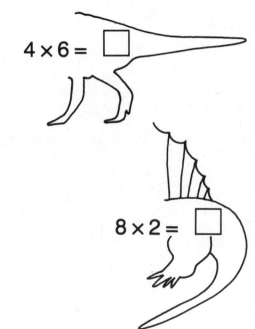

$8 \times 2 = \square$

4	8	3	5	9	8	7	9
$\times 7$	$\times 6$	$\times 4$	$\times 7$	$\times 5$	$\times 4$	$\times 7$	$\times 6$

5	8	7	6	9	3	8	7
$\times 6$	$\times 7$	$\times 4$	$\times 5$	$\times 7$	$\times 7$	$\times 5$	$\times 5$

Basic Math Skills 3

Why did the dinosaur wear blue sneakers?

16-t	35-a	48-h
18-k	36-n	49-p
24-e	40-r	56-s
32-i	42-w	64-o

8 ×6	6 ×4	8 ×5

7 ×7	4 ×8	9 ×4	9 ×2

8 ×8	6 ×6	3 ×8	8 ×7

6 ×7	4 ×6	8 ×5	8 ×3

8 ×4	4 ×9

4 ×4	6 ×8	8 ×3

7 ×6	5 ×7	7 ×8	8 ×6

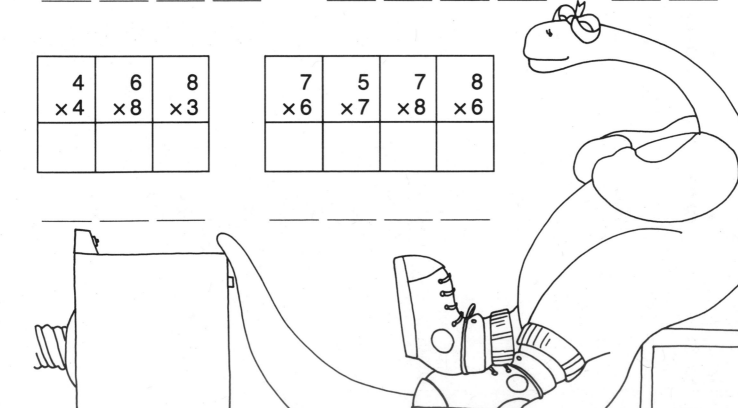

Basic Math Skills 3

Styracosaurus

Start at 0.

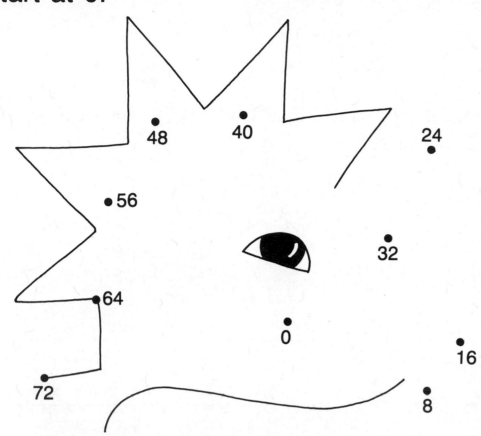

$0 \times 8 =$ _____
$1 \times 8 =$ _____
$2 \times 8 =$ _____
$3 \times 8 =$ _____
$4 \times 8 =$ _____
$5 \times 8 =$ _____
$6 \times 8 =$ _____
$7 \times 8 =$ _____
$8 \times 8 =$ _____
$9 \times 8 =$ _____

| 0 | 2 | 1 | 4 | 3 | 5 | 4 | 5 |
| $\times 8$ | $\times 6$ | $\times 8$ | $\times 7$ | $\times 8$ | $\times 5$ | $\times 6$ | $\times 8$ |

| 2 | 5 | 6 | 3 | 8 | 7 | 2 | 4 |
| $\times 8$ | $\times 7$ | $\times 8$ | $\times 6$ | $\times 7$ | $\times 8$ | $\times 7$ | $\times 8$ |

| 9 | 8 | 6 | 4 | 9 | 3 | 6 | 9 |
| $\times 3$ | $\times 8$ | $\times 7$ | $\times 5$ | $\times 8$ | $\times 3$ | $\times 5$ | $\times 7$ |

 Basic Math Skills 3

Dinosaur Marathon

1 ×6	2 ×8	0 ×7	2 ×6	0 ×8	1 ×8	2 ×7	1 ×7
3 ×6	5 ×5	6 ×6	3 ×3	7 ×6	6 ×3	8 ×8	3 ×7
6 ×7	4 ×6	2 ×5	9 ×6	4 ×7	4 ×4	6 ×8	7 ×7
7 ×8	6 ×3	5 ×6	3 ×2	8 ×4	9 ×2	1 ×4	7 ×3
8 ×7	1 ×1	3 ×8	0 ×3	6 ×6	7 ×3	5 ×8	5 ×7
7 ×5	4 ×8	5 ×2	4 ×3	9 ×8	8 ×6	3 ×5	9 ×7

Basic Math Skills 3

A Styracosaurus had large horns and a huge shield on its head. These were for protection. Styracosaurus means "spiked lizard."

6 ×4	5 ×7	7 ×8	8 ×3	5 ×2	9 ×8	8 ×2	5 ×3
9 ×4	8 ×8	3 ×7	5 ×8	0 ×6	5 ×7	6 ×6	8 ×7
4 ×8	6 ×7	3 ×5	9 ×7	7 ×2	8 ×4	6 ×5	5 ×4
5 ×6	7 ×3	8 ×6	9 ×2	7 ×6	6 ×3	5 ×5	9 ×6
3 ×6	9 ×5	2 ×5	7 ×4	3 ×7	6 ×8	4 ×2	7 ×7

Basic Math Skills 3

Who Am I?

0-s	16-n	36-k
6-r	24-u	42-b
8-o	28-g	49-m
12-a	30-t	56-y
14-l	32-e	

$\begin{array}{r}8\\\times4\end{array}$	$\begin{array}{r}2\\\times7\end{array}$	$\begin{array}{r}4\\\times3\end{array}$	$\begin{array}{r}0\\\times2\end{array}$	$\begin{array}{r}7\\\times7\end{array}$	$\begin{array}{r}8\\\times1\end{array}$	$\begin{array}{r}8\\\times0\end{array}$	$\begin{array}{r}6\\\times2\end{array}$	$\begin{array}{r}3\\\times8\end{array}$	$\begin{array}{r}2\\\times3\end{array}$	$\begin{array}{r}6\\\times4\end{array}$	$\begin{array}{r}0\\\times5\end{array}$

$\begin{array}{r}0\\\times7\end{array}$	$\begin{array}{r}5\\\times6\end{array}$	$\begin{array}{r}4\\\times8\end{array}$	$\begin{array}{r}7\\\times4\end{array}$	$\begin{array}{r}2\\\times4\end{array}$	$\begin{array}{r}6\\\times0\end{array}$	$\begin{array}{r}2\\\times6\end{array}$	$\begin{array}{r}8\\\times3\end{array}$	$\begin{array}{r}2\\\times3\end{array}$	$\begin{array}{r}6\\\times4\end{array}$	$\begin{array}{r}0\\\times3\end{array}$

What did the mother dinosaur say when she looked at her egg?

8-o	21-r	36-i
12-s	24-t	40-u
15-a	25-c	42-b
16-e	28-n	45-g
18-h	30-d	49-m
20-f	35-l	

6 ×4	9 ×2	6 ×6	6 ×2

5 ×5	4 ×2	8 ×5	5 ×7	6 ×5

7 ×6	8 ×2

8 ×3	2 ×9	4 ×4

4 ×3	4 ×6	5 ×3	3 ×7	3 ×8

2 ×4	4 ×5

3 ×4	8 ×1	7 ×7	2 ×8	8 ×3	6 ×3	4 ×9	7 ×4	9 ×5

6 ×7	9 ×4	5 ×9

_____ _____ _____ _____ !

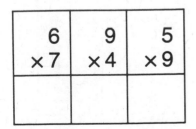

Basic Math Skills 3

Match the eggs to the dinosaurs.

$2 \times 9 =$ ☐

$6 \times 2 =$ ☐

$3 \times 2 =$ ☐

$8 \times 1 =$ ☐

$1 \times 6 =$ ☐

$3 \times 6 =$ ☐

$8 \times 3 =$ ☐

$4 \times 6 =$ ☐

$4 \times 3 =$ ☐

$4 \times 2 =$ ☐

6

8

12

18

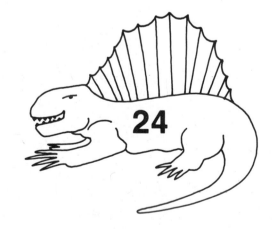

24

$6 \times 3 =$ ☐

$3 \times 4 =$ ☐

$9 \times 2 =$ ☐

$6 \times 1 =$ ☐

$2 \times 3 =$ ☐

$2 \times 4 =$ ☐

$6 \times 4 =$ ☐

$1 \times 8 =$ ☐

$2 \times 6 =$ ☐

$3 \times 8 =$ ☐

Basic Math Skills 3

Cut and paste to find the hidden dinosaur.

5 ×7	8 ×8	2 ×9	7 ×9	4 ×9	6 ×8
4 ×8	8 ×9	3 ×9	6 ×7	5 ×8	7 ×7
9 ×9	2 ×8	7 ×8	4 ×7	6 ×9	5 ×9

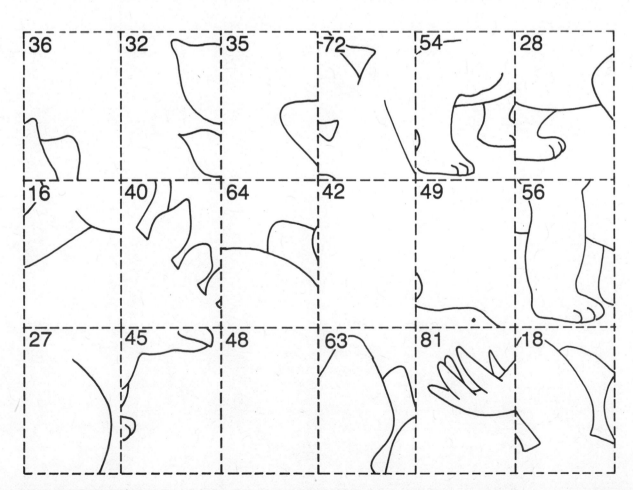

A Compsognathus had long legs, bird like feet, and sharp claws. It was one of the small dinosaurs. It was only about two feet long.

$0 \times 9 =$ $1 \times 7 =$ $3 \times 8 =$
$9 \times 0 =$ $7 \times 1 =$ $8 \times 3 =$

$4 \times 7 =$ $9 \times 8 =$ $6 \times 9 =$
$7 \times 4 =$ $8 \times 9 =$ $9 \times 6 =$

$5 \times 8 =$ $9 \times 7 =$ $6 \times 8 =$
$8 \times 5 =$ $7 \times 9 =$ $8 \times 6 =$

$5 \times 9 =$ $3 \times 7 =$ $4 \times 9 =$
$9 \times 5 =$ $7 \times 3 =$ $9 \times 4 =$

$8 \times 7 =$ $9 \times 3 =$ $6 \times 7 =$
$7 \times 8 =$ $3 \times 9 =$ $7 \times 6 =$

$6 \times 3 =$ $7 \times 5 =$ $4 \times 8 =$
$3 \times 6 =$ $5 \times 7 =$ $8 \times 4 =$

$9 \times 9 =$ $8 \times 8 =$ $7 \times 7 =$

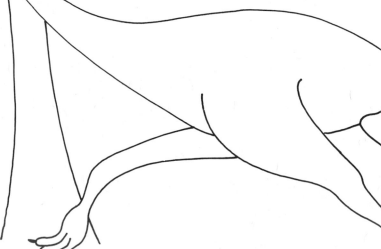

Basic Math Skills 3

Help the dinosaur escape.

Color these answers **brown** to find the escape path.

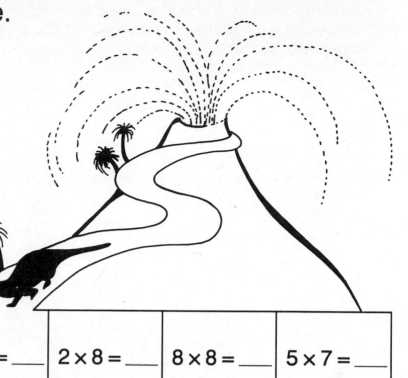

18   24   36

7 × 9 = ___	2 × 6 = ___	4 × 9 = ___	2 × 8 = ___	8 × 8 = ___	5 × 7 = ___
6 × 7 = ___	3 × 7 = ___	3 × 6 = ___	6 × 4 = ___	9 × 2 = ___	7 × 8 = ___
7 × 7 = ___	9 × 9 = ___	6 × 8 = ___	4 × 8 = ___	9 × 4 = ___	6 × 9 = ___
9 × 8 = ___	4 × 9 = ___	6 × 6 = ___	8 × 3 = ___	9 × 4 = ___	6 × 9 = ___
6 × 3 = ___	3 × 8 = ___	5 × 9 = ___	9 × 7 = ___	6 × 5 = ___	8 × 4 = ___
4 × 6 = ___	8 × 7 = ___	9 × 6 = ___	7 × 6 = ___	5 × 7 = ___	9 × 8 = ___

Basic Math Skills 3

Start at 0:

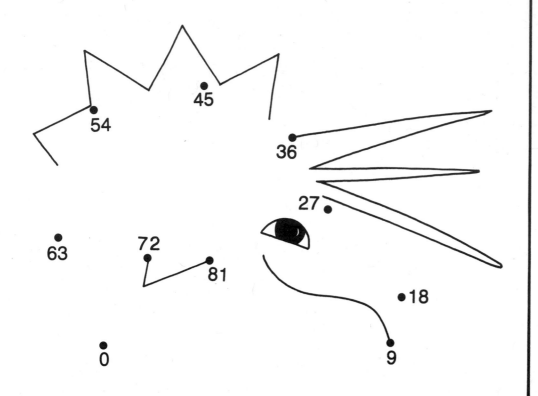

$0 \times 9 = \underline{\hspace{1cm}}$

$1 \times 9 = \underline{\hspace{1cm}}$

$2 \times 9 = \underline{\hspace{1cm}}$

$3 \times 9 = \underline{\hspace{1cm}}$

$4 \times 9 = \underline{\hspace{1cm}}$

$5 \times 9 = \underline{\hspace{1cm}}$

$6 \times 9 = \underline{\hspace{1cm}}$

$7 \times 9 = \underline{\hspace{1cm}}$

$8 \times 9 = \underline{\hspace{1cm}}$

$9 \times 9 = \underline{\hspace{1cm}}$

2	3	0	7	1	4	5	9
×8	×9	×9	×8	×9	×9	×8	×5

2	0	1	5	3	5	9	6
×9	×8	×8	×9	×8	×9	×9	×8

8	4	9	8	9	9	8	6
×9	×8	×6	×7	×8	×7	×8	×9

Basic Math Skills 3

Color the answers to find the missing dinosaur.

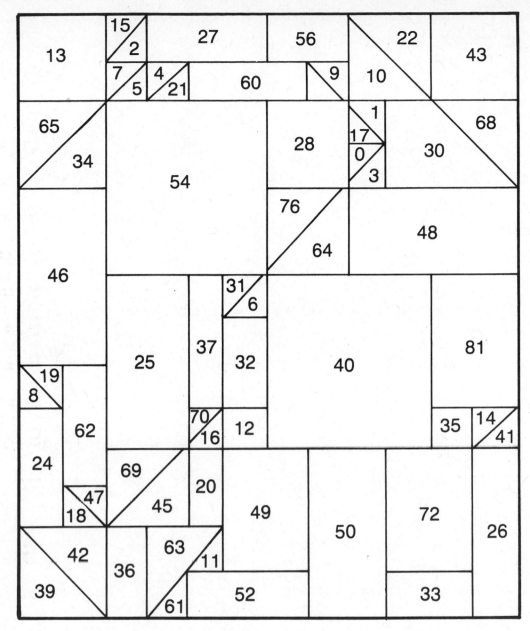

1	2	3	2	5	2	6	3
×1	×1	×3	×2	×1	×3	×2	×1

1	2	2	4	2	3	2	3
×7	×4	×5	×5	×9	×9	×7	×8

4	2	5	6	4	5	5	6
×9	×8	×9	×5	×8	×7	×8	×7

9	7	6	8	8	7	8
×9	×7	×8	×9	×7	×9	×8

Basic Math Skills 3

Color the toy dinosaur.

64 — yellow stripes
75 — yellow
96 — red dots
99 — red
108 — green
120 — green dots
136 — orange
189 — orange stripes

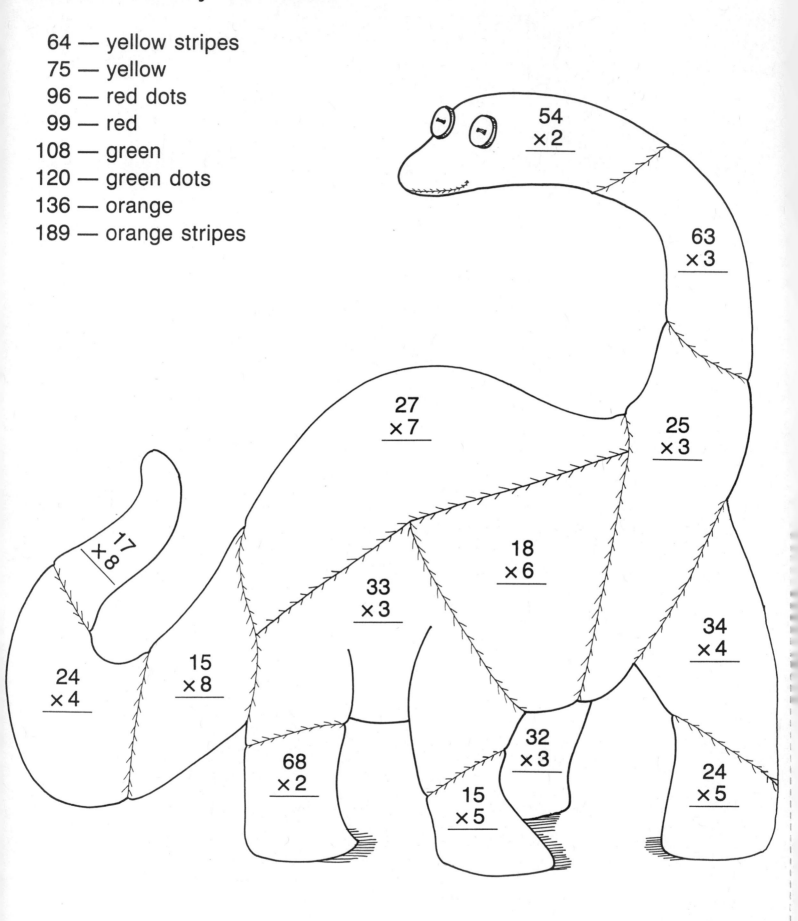

Basic Math Skills 3

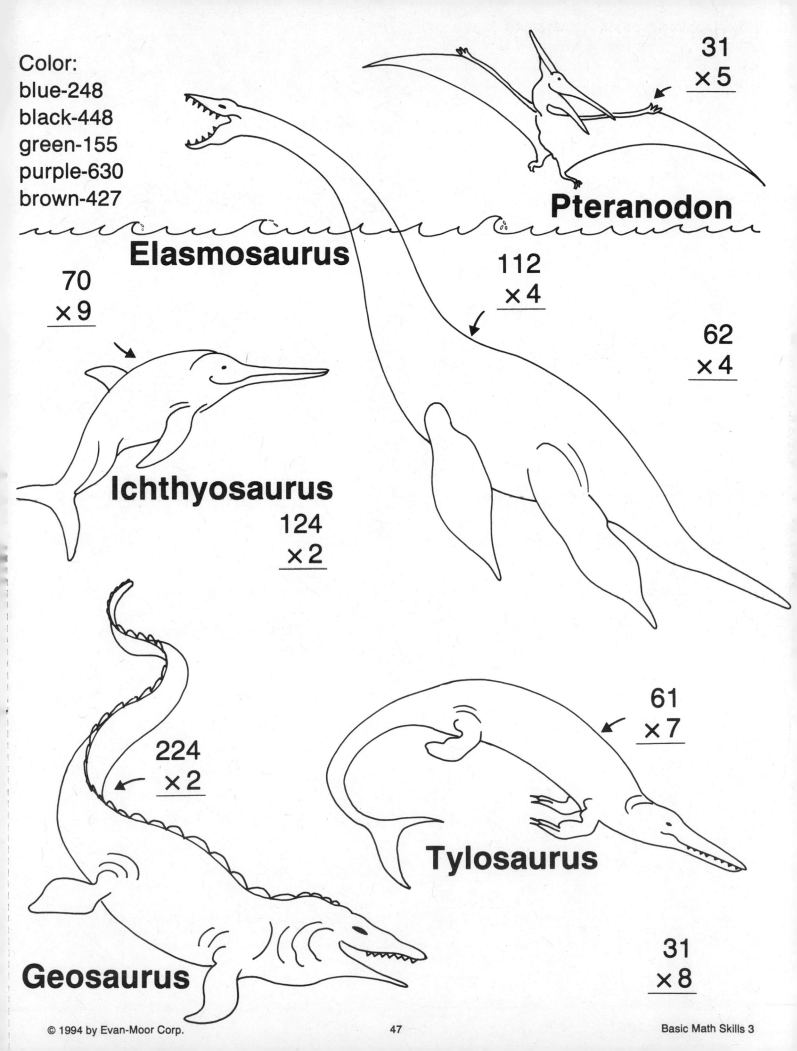

Color:
blue-248
black-448
green-155
purple-630
brown-427

Pteranodon

31
×5

Elasmosaurus

70
×9

112
×4

62
×4

Ichthyosaurus

124
×2

224
×2

61
×7

Tylosaurus

Geosaurus

31
×8

Basic Math Skills 3

Coelophysis was an active meat eater. It was not very big. It was built for speed with a long, slender neck, bird-like feet, and hollow bones.

$$64 \times 2$$ $$83 \times 3$$

$$72 \times 4$$ $$50 \times 8$$ $$97 \times 1$$ $$432 \times 2$$

$$51 \times 5$$ $$39 \times 2$$ $$65 \times 4$$ $$38 \times 3$$ $$124 \times 6$$

$$27 \times 8$$ $$45 \times 9$$ $$86 \times 7$$ $$75 \times 5$$ $$243 \times 4$$

Bonus:

$$139 \times 5$$ $$265 \times 8$$ $$643 \times 7$$ $$582 \times 9$$ $$634 \times 6$$

Basic Math Skills 3

Name _____

Timed Test

5 ×0	4 ×0	1 ×1	2 ×2	5 ×3	6 ×5
2 ×3	2 ×0	5 ×1	6 ×3	4 ×3	4 ×5
9 ×3	3 ×2	3 ×0	4 ×1	3 ×3	6 ×2
1 ×0	7 ×2	4 ×2	0 ×0	2 ×1	8 ×3
5 ×2	3 ×1	7 ×3	5 ×5	9 ×2	8 ×2

Basic Math Skills 3

Name _____

Timed Test

Time	Number Correct
2 min.	
1 min.	

$$\begin{array}{c} 0 \\ \times 6 \\ \hline \end{array} \qquad \begin{array}{c} 1 \\ \times 7 \\ \hline \end{array} \qquad \begin{array}{c} 4 \\ \times 9 \\ \hline \end{array} \qquad \begin{array}{c} 2 \\ \times 6 \\ \hline \end{array} \qquad \begin{array}{c} 3 \\ \times 7 \\ \hline \end{array} \qquad \begin{array}{c} 8 \\ \times 4 \\ \hline \end{array}$$

$$\begin{array}{c} 6 \\ \times 6 \\ \hline \end{array} \qquad \begin{array}{c} 5 \\ \times 7 \\ \hline \end{array} \qquad \begin{array}{c} 4 \\ \times 8 \\ \hline \end{array} \qquad \begin{array}{c} 0 \\ \times 9 \\ \hline \end{array} \qquad \begin{array}{c} 6 \\ \times 9 \\ \hline \end{array} \qquad \begin{array}{c} 4 \\ \times 6 \\ \hline \end{array}$$

$$\begin{array}{c} 7 \\ \times 7 \\ \hline \end{array} \qquad \begin{array}{c} 4 \\ \times 7 \\ \hline \end{array} \qquad \begin{array}{c} 3 \\ \times 8 \\ \hline \end{array} \qquad \begin{array}{c} 1 \\ \times 8 \\ \hline \end{array} \qquad \begin{array}{c} 3 \\ \times 6 \\ \hline \end{array} \qquad \begin{array}{c} 2 \\ \times 9 \\ \hline \end{array}$$

$$\begin{array}{c} 5 \\ \times 9 \\ \hline \end{array} \qquad \begin{array}{c} 2 \\ \times 8 \\ \hline \end{array} \qquad \begin{array}{c} 6 \\ \times 6 \\ \hline \end{array} \qquad \begin{array}{c} 6 \\ \times 3 \\ \hline \end{array} \qquad \begin{array}{c} 1 \\ \times 9 \\ \hline \end{array} \qquad \begin{array}{c} 2 \\ \times 7 \\ \hline \end{array}$$

$$\begin{array}{c} 7 \\ \times 3 \\ \hline \end{array} \qquad \begin{array}{c} 0 \\ \times 8 \\ \hline \end{array} \qquad \begin{array}{c} 5 \\ \times 6 \\ \hline \end{array} \qquad \begin{array}{c} 2 \\ \times 7 \\ \hline \end{array} \qquad \begin{array}{c} 5 \\ \times 8 \\ \hline \end{array} \qquad \begin{array}{c} 2 \\ \times 9 \\ \hline \end{array}$$

Basic Math Skills 3

Beginning Division

The following pages help students practice these basic division skills:

- *dividing by one-digit numbers 1-9*

- *recognizing division symbols in three forms*

  $2\overline{)4}$ $4 \div 2$ $\dfrac{4}{2}$

- *checking division by multiplying*

Answer Key

Page 53:
```
2   3   1
5   9   6
8   4   7
5   3   8
7   1   6
4   9   2
```

Page 54:
```
6   3
9   5
6   8
    3
    8
    4
    9
    4
    5
```

Page 55:
```
1   2
4   8
5   9
6   7
3   8   6
7   2   4
1   9   5
```

Page 56:
```
5   1   6
9   7   3
8   4   2
3   5   8
2   1   9
6   4   7
```

Page 57:
```
1   5
2   2
8   5
3   3
4   1
9   4
7   8
9   7
9   5   4
6   8
```

Page 58:
```
4   9   3
8   5   7
2   6   1
7   1   3
9   5   8
6   4   2
```

Page 59:
```
1   6   4
5   3   8
2   7   9
4   7   1
8   9   5
2   6   3
```

Page 60:
```
5   7   4
9   8   2
6   3   11
4   1   7
2   9   5
6   8   3
```

Page 61:

Page 62:
```
2   4   9
6   8   5
3   1   7
4   8
6   7
9   5
2   3
```

Page 63:
```
5   5
8   8
3   3
7   7
9   9
4   4
```

Page 64:
```
3
3
7
8
3
6
```

Page 65:
(timed test)
```
1   2   2   9   2   1
8   6   4   8   5   2
6   3   1   5   6   1
9   1   3   4   6   9
9   1   4   5   7   8
```

Page 66:
(timed test)
```
3   3   7   6   9   8
5   7   3   8   5   8
7   7   4   9   6   6
5   4   7   7   6   8
9   7   4   5   9   9
```

Page 67:
(timed test)
```
2   1   2   2   3   6
5   3   4   4   3   2
4   6   8   7   4   8
7   9   6   6   5   9
9   5   8   9   8   5
```

Page 68:
(timed test)
```
1   5   1   3   3   4
7   7   1   6   6   5
8   2   3   9   9   3
8   7   4   9   2   6
5   6   8   4   7   5
```

Basic Math Skills 3

Did you know these mean the same thing?

Divide by 2.

$4 \div 2 = 2$ $6 \div 2 = \underline{}$ $2 \div 2 = \underline{}$

$10 \div 2 = \underline{}$ $18 \div 2 = \underline{}$ $12 \div 2 = \underline{}$

$16 \div 2 = \underline{}$ $8 \div 2 = \underline{}$ $14 \div 2 = \underline{}$

Now try to divide this way.

$2 \overline{)10}$ $2 \overline{)6}$ $2 \overline{)16}$

$2 \overline{)14}$ $2 \overline{)2}$ $2 \overline{)12}$

$2 \overline{)8}$ $2 \overline{)18}$ $2 \overline{)4}$

               Basic Math Skills 3

Check division
by multiplying.

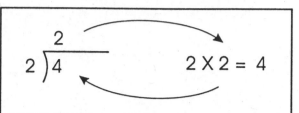

$$2 \times 2 = 4$$

3 X __3__ = 9	3)9
3 X ___ = 15	3)15
2 X ___ = 16	2)16
2 X ___ = 6	2)6
3 X ___ = 24	3)24
2 X ___ = 8	2)8

3 X ___ = 18	3)18	3 X ___ = 27	3)27
2 X ___ = 18	2)18	3 X ___ = 12	3)12
2 X ___ = 12	2)12	2 X ___ = 10	2)10

Basic Math Skills 3

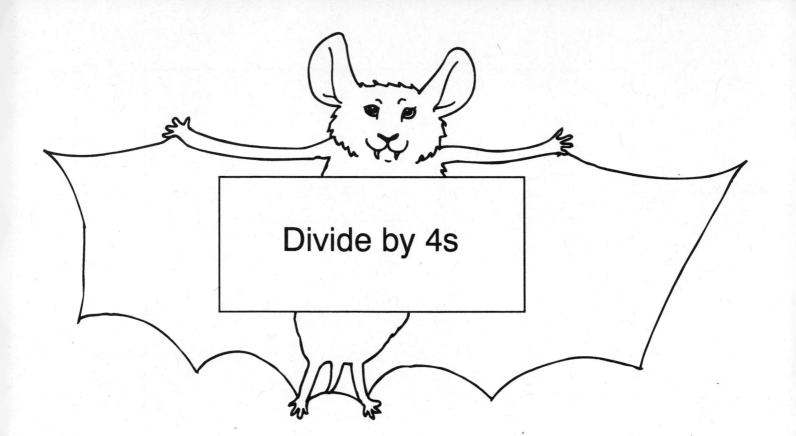

Divide by 4s

$4 \div 4 = \_\_\_$ $8 \div 4 = \_\_\_$

$16 \div 4 = \_\_\_$ $32 \div 4 = \_\_\_$

$20 \div 4 = \_\_\_$ $36 \div 4 = \_\_\_$

$24 \div 4 = \_\_\_$ $28 \div 4 = \_\_\_$

$4 \overline{)12}$ $4 \overline{)32}$ $4 \overline{)24}$

$4 \overline{)28}$ $4 \overline{)8}$ $4 \overline{)16}$

$4 \overline{)4}$ $4 \overline{)36}$ $4 \overline{)20}$

Basic Math Skills 3

Do you know the "fives"?

$$5 \overline{)25} \qquad 5 \overline{)5} \qquad 5 \overline{)30}$$

$$5 \overline{)45} \qquad 5 \overline{)35} \qquad 5 \overline{)15}$$

$$5 \overline{)40} \qquad 5 \overline{)20} \qquad 5 \overline{)10}$$

$15 \div 5 = \boxed{}$ $25 \div 5 = \boxed{}$ $40 \div 5 = \boxed{}$

$10 \div 5 = \boxed{}$ $5 \div 5 = \boxed{}$ $45 \div 5 = \boxed{}$

$30 \div 5 = \boxed{}$ $20 \div 5 = \boxed{}$ $35 \div 5 = \boxed{}$

Review

$3 \div 3 = \square$

$15 \div 3 = \square$

$6 \div 3 = \square$ $8 \div 4 = \square$

$24 \div 3 = \square$ $20 \div 4 = \square$

$9 \div 3 = \square$ $12 \div 4 = \square$

$12 \div 3 = \square$ $4 \div 4 = \square$

$27 \div 3 = \square$ $16 \div 4 = \square$

$21 \div 3 = \square$ $32 \div 4 = \square$

$36 \div 4 = \square$ $28 \div 4 = \square$

$5 \overline{)45}$ $5 \overline{)25}$ $5 \overline{)20}$

$5 \overline{)30}$ $5 \overline{)40}$

          Basic Math Skills 3

Do you know your "sixes"?

Divide by 6.

24 ÷ 6 = ___	54 ÷ 6 = ___	18 ÷ 6 = ___
48 ÷ 6 = ___	30 ÷ 6 = ___	42 ÷ 6 = ___
12 ÷ 6 = ___	36 ÷ 6 = ___	6 ÷ 6 = ___

Now try to divide this way.

6)42	6)6	6)18
6)54	6)30	6)48
6)36	6)24	6)12

Do you know the "sevens"?

$7\overline{)7}$ $7\overline{)42}$ $7\overline{)28}$

$7\overline{)35}$ $7\overline{)21}$ $7\overline{)56}$

$7\overline{)14}$ $7\overline{)49}$ $7\overline{)63}$

$28 \div 7 = \Box$ $49 \div 7 = \Box$ $7 \div 7 = \Box$

$56 \div 7 = \Box$ $63 \div 7 = \Box$ $35 \div 7 = \Box$

$14 \div 7 = \Box$ $42 \div 7 = \Box$ $21 \div 7 = \Box$

Basic Math Skills 3

Do you know the "eights"?

$40 \div 8 = \boxed{}$ $56 \div 8 = \boxed{}$ $32 \div 8 = \boxed{}$

$72 \div 8 = \boxed{}$ $64 \div 8 = \boxed{}$ $16 \div 8 = \boxed{}$

$48 \div 8 = \boxed{}$ $24 \div 8 = \boxed{}$ $88 \div 8 = \boxed{}$

$8\overline{)32}$ $8\overline{)8}$ $8\overline{)56}$

$8\overline{)16}$ $8\overline{)72}$ $8\overline{)40}$

$8\overline{)48}$ $8\overline{)64}$ $8\overline{)24}$

Basic Math Skills 3

Help the bat find its cave by drawing a line to connect all answers of 8.

start here

2)16	1)8	8)72	8)32
8)40	3)24	8)56	8)48
7)63	7)56	6)54	8)16
7)35	6)48	8)64	5)40
6)30	8)24	8)8	4)32

cave

Basic Math Skills 3

Do you know the "nines"?

$9\overline{)18}$ $9\overline{)36}$ $9\overline{)81}$

$9\overline{)54}$ $9\overline{)72}$ $9\overline{)45}$

$9\overline{)27}$ $9\overline{)9}$ $9\overline{)63}$

$36 \div 9 =$ ___ $72 \div 9 =$ ___

$54 \div 9 =$ ___ $63 \div 9 =$ ___

$81 \div 9 =$ ___ $45 \div 9 =$ ___

$18 \div 9 =$ ___ $27 \div 9 =$ ___

Basic Math Skills 3

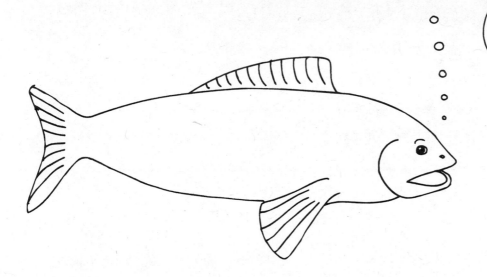

Check division by multiplying.

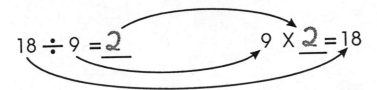

$18 \div 9 = \underline{2}$ $9 \times \underline{2} = 18$

$45 \div 9 = \underline{}$ $9 \times \underline{} = 45$

$72 \div 9 = \underline{}$ $9 \times \underline{} = 72$

$27 \div 9 = \underline{}$ $9 \times \underline{} = 27$

$63 \div 9 = \underline{}$ $9 \times \underline{} = 63$

$81 \div 9 = \underline{}$ $9 \times \underline{} = 81$

$36 \div 9 = \underline{}$ $9 \times \underline{} = 36$

 Basic Math Skills 3

Three Ways to Divide

$$2\overline{)4} \; = \; 4 \div 2 \; = \; \frac{4}{2} \; = \; 2$$

$4\overline{)12} \; = \; 12 \div 4 \; = \; \dfrac{12}{4} \; = \; \square$

$\boxed{\overline{)}} \; = \; 9 \div 3 \; = \; \dfrac{9}{3} \; = \; \square$

$5\overline{)35} \; = \; \boxed{\div} \; = \; \dfrac{35}{5} \; = \; \square$

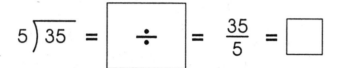

$2\overline{)16} \; = \; 16 \div 2 \; = \; \boxed{\;-\;} \; = \; \square$

$8\overline{)24} \; = \; \boxed{\div} \; = \; \dfrac{24}{8} \; = \; \square$

$9\overline{)54} \; = \; 54 \div 9 \; = \; \boxed{\;-\;} \; = \; \square$

Basic Math Skills 3

Name _____

Time	Number Correct
2 min.	
1 min.	

Timed Test

$1 \overline{)1}$ $2 \overline{)4}$ $3 \overline{)6}$ $1 \overline{)9}$ $4 \overline{)8}$ $5 \overline{)5}$

$4 \overline{)32}$ $2 \overline{)12}$ $4 \overline{)16}$ $3 \overline{)24}$ $3 \overline{)15}$ $5 \overline{)10}$

$1 \overline{)6}$ $3 \overline{)9}$ $3 \overline{)3}$ $2 \overline{)10}$ $4 \overline{)24}$ $4 \overline{)4}$

$3 \overline{)27}$ $3 \overline{)3}$ $2 \overline{)6}$ $3 \overline{)12}$ $3 \overline{)18}$ $4 \overline{)36}$

$2 \overline{)18}$ $6 \overline{)6}$ $2 \overline{)8}$ $1 \overline{)5}$ $3 \overline{)21}$ $2 \overline{)16}$

       Basic Math Skills 3

Time	Number Correct
2 min.	
1 min.	

Timed Test

$6\overline{)18}$ $\quad$ $8\overline{)24}$ $\quad$ $6\overline{)42}$ $\quad$ $9\overline{)54}$ $\quad$ $8\overline{)72}$ $\quad$ $6\overline{)48}$

$9\overline{)45}$ $\quad$ $7\overline{)49}$ $\quad$ $7\overline{)21}$ $\quad$ $8\overline{)64}$ $\quad$ $6\overline{)30}$ $\quad$ $7\overline{)56}$

$7\overline{)49}$ $\quad$ $6\overline{)42}$ $\quad$ $7\overline{)28}$ $\quad$ $7\overline{)63}$ $\quad$ $6\overline{)36}$ $\quad$ $8\overline{)48}$

$8\overline{)40}$ $\quad$ $6\overline{)24}$ $\quad$ $9\overline{)63}$ $\quad$ $8\overline{)56}$ $\quad$ $7\overline{)42}$ $\quad$ $9\overline{)72}$

$7\overline{)63}$ $\quad$ $9\overline{)63}$ $\quad$ $9\overline{)36}$ $\quad$ $7\overline{)35}$ $\quad$ $6\overline{)54}$ $\quad$ $9\overline{)81}$

   Basic Math Skills 3

Name _____

Timed Test

	Time	Number Correct
2 min.		
1 min.		

7)14   6)6   9)18   8)16   6)18   8)48

6)30   7)21   8)32   7)28   9)27   6)12

6)24   7)42   7)56   6)42   9)36   8)64

8)56   8)72   6)36   9)54   7)35   6)54

8)72   9)45   6)48   9)81   9)72   8)40

67   Basic Math Skills 3

Name _____

Time	Number Correct
2 min.	
1 min.	

Timed Test

$2\overline{)2}$ $3\overline{)15}$ $4\overline{)4}$ $3\overline{)9}$ $2\overline{)6}$ $3\overline{)12}$

$2\overline{)14}$ $3\overline{)21}$ $5\overline{)5}$ $3\overline{)18}$ $2\overline{)12}$ $2\overline{)10}$

$3\overline{)24}$ $4\overline{)8}$ $5\overline{)15}$ $2\overline{)18}$ $5\overline{)45}$ $4\overline{)12}$

$5\overline{)40}$ $5\overline{)35}$ $4\overline{)16}$ $3\overline{)27}$ $2\overline{)4}$ $4\overline{)24}$

$4\overline{)20}$ $5\overline{)30}$ $4\overline{)32}$ $5\overline{)20}$ $4\overline{)28}$ $5\overline{)25}$

68   Basic Math Skills 3

Telling Time
Tell Time to the Minute

These pages provide students with practice in telling time to the minute.

- *Reading Clocks*

- *Writing Times*

- *Word Problems*

- *Before and After*

Answer Key

Page 71
4:00	6:00	2:00
11:00	3:00	12:00
2:30	5:30	3:30
11:30	7:30	6:30

Page 72 See Clock faces.

Page 73
A. 3:00 B. 8:00 C. 4:30 D. 5:30
E. 5:00 F. 6:00 G. 7:30
H.—J. Answers will vary.

Page 74
1. 5:00 2. 2 hours 3. 7:30 4. 4 hours
5. 4:00 6. 6:00 7. 2 hours, 30 minutes
8. 2 hours, 30 minutes

Page 75
A. 9:45 E. 7:15
B. 3:15 F. 5:45
C. 8:45 G. 11:45
D. 10:45 H. 6:15

Page 76 See clock faces.

Page 77
2:15 1:15 6:15
15 min. after 2 15 min. after 1 15 min. after 6
11:45 5:45 8:45
15 min. until 12 15 min. until 6 15 min. until 9
10:45 7:15 2:15
3:45 12:15 9:45

Page 78
5, 10, 15, 20, 25, 30, 35, 40, 45, 50, 55
4:05 4:30 4:10
4:55 4:25 4:40

Page 79
A. 2:20 F. 3:05
B. 8:05 G. 7:35
C. 9:25 H. 6:55
D. 10:30 I. 1:50
E. 5:40 J. 6:55

Page 80
5:10 7:05 10:20
4:30 2:45 5:35
8:50 10:15 6:25
3:55 1:40 9:00

Page 81 See clock faces.

Page 82 Answers will vary.

Page 83
A. 9:35 E. 2:30 I. 4:25 M. 4:55
B. 9:40 F. 2:50 J. 6:20 N. 6:20
C. 6:45 G. 9:05 K. 10:30 O. 10:40
D. 6:55 H. 9:40 L. 2:45 P. 1:45

Page 84 Count 1 to 60 60 minutes 30 minutes

Page 85
A. 11 B. 18 C. 4
D. 14 E. 27 F. 24
G. 34 H. 49 I. 44

Page 86
A. 7:04 E. 8:23
B. 6:19 F. 4:37
C. 3:42 G. 1:26
D. 11:02 H. 10:54

Page 87
8:09 8:22 8:41
8:03 8:53 8:11
8:17 8:27 8:18

Page 88
4:28	6:47	3:18
9:12	8:34	10:07
5:24	12:00	12:18
7:39	5:03	1:45

Page 89 See clock faces.

Page 90
1. 20 minutes 2. build a model 3. 6:40 4. 6:30
   45 minutes   catch a ball
   55 minutes
5. and 6. Answers wil vary.

Page 91
1. 25 minutes 6. 4:58
2. 45 minutes 7. 5:10
3. 10 minutes 8. 6:28
4. 2:58 9. 9:30
5. 50 minutes

Page 92
1. A.M. 5. P.M. 9. A.M.
2. P.M. 6. A.M. 10. A.M.
3. P.M. 7. P.M. 11. P.M.
4. A.M. 8. P.M. 12. A.M.

Page 93
1. Tweeter—10:45 2. 45 minutes
   Patches— 3:00 3. 9:35
   Speedy— 2:30 4. 4:45
5. 8 hours, 15 minutes

Page 94
1. 12 minutes 2. 6:37 3. 200 bounces 4. 4:03
5. 6 airplanes 6. 3:31 7. 36 minutes 8. 1:51

Page 95
1. 1:00 2. 7:55 3. 10:32
4. 3:10 5. 3:30 6. 7:05

Page 96 Answers will vary.

Page 97
1. 2 minutes 2. 3 hours 3. 2 days
   300 seconds 240 minutes 72 hours
   4 minutes ½ hour 120 hours
4. 3 weeks 5. 2 years 6. 520 weeks
   63 days 156 weeks
   5 weeks 260 weeks
Bonus—168 hours Super Bonus—10,080 minutes

Page 98
3:00, 5:00 5:30, 6:30 7:00, 11:00 7:00, 7:20
7:30, 9:30 12:00, 1:00 4:10, 8:10 9:30, 9:50
10:15, 12:15 9:15,10:15 2:37, 6:37 11:15, 11:35
1:06, 3:06 6:55, 7:55 12:30, 4:30 3:20, 3:40
2:58, 4:58 9:45,10:45 9:00, 1:00 5:05, 5:25

Page 99
1. Pacific, Mountain, Central, Eastern
2. 2:00 Utah 3:00 Missouri
   4:00 Florida 1:00 Oregon
   3:00 Iowa 4:00 Maine
3. 3:15
4. 1 hour
5. 11:00

Page 100
A. 1. 9:00 2. 2:30 3. 6:15 4. 4:45
   5. 3:03 6. 5:41 7. 7:59 8. 11:18
B. See clock faces.
C. 1. P.M. 2. P.M. 3. A.M. 4. A.M.
D. 60 minutes 24 hours 7 days 52 weeks

Basic Math Skills 3

What time is it?

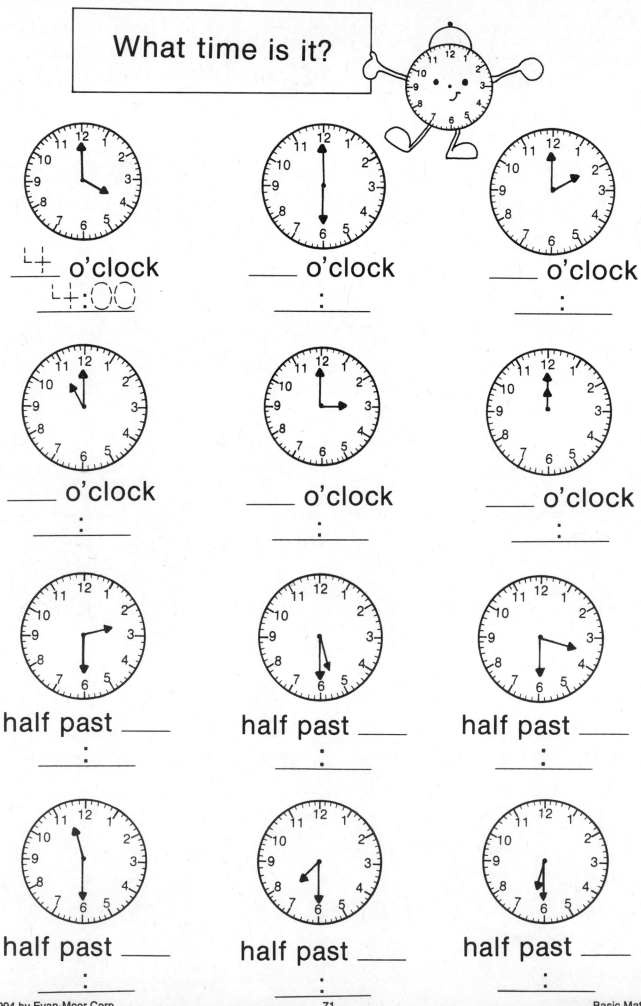

____4____ o'clock

____4:00____

____ o'clock
_____:_____

____ o'clock
_____:_____

____ o'clock
_____:_____

____ o'clock
_____:_____

____ o'clock
_____:_____

half past ____
_____:_____

half past ____
_____:_____

half past ____
_____:_____

half past ____
_____:_____

half past ____
_____:_____

half past ____
_____:_____

 Put the hands on the clock faces.

3 o'clock

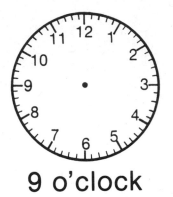

9 o'clock

1 o'clock

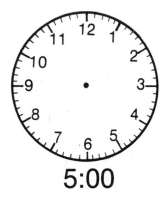

5:00

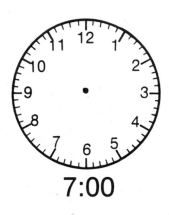

7:00

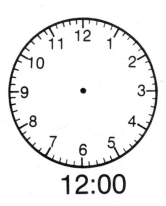

12:00

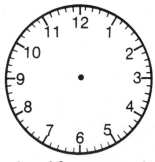

half past 4

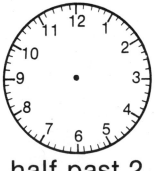

half past 2

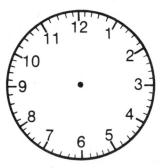

half past 6

10:30

8:30

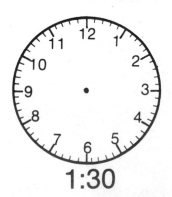

1:30

Basic Math Skills 3

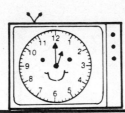 TV Time

Title	Show begins	Show lasts	Show ends
A. Zoo Parade	2:00	1 hour	___:___
B. Top Ten Music Hour	___:___	1 hour	9:00
C. Uncle Will's Magic Show	4:00	30 minutes	___:___
D. P.M. News	___:___	30 minutes	6:00
E. Cartoon Time	3:00	2 hours	___:___
F. Movie Theater	___:___	2 hours	8:00
G. Jungle Adventure	6:00	1 hour 30 minutes	___:___

H. What is your favorite TV show? _____

I. When does it come on? _____

J. How long does it last? ____ hours ____ minutes

73 Basic Math Skills 3

Think About It

1. Concert
   begins 2:00
   lasts 3 hours
   ends __5:00__

2. Soccer Game
   begins 1:30
   lasts _____ hours
   ends 3:30

3. Party
   begins 3:30
   lasts 4 hours
   ends ___:___

4. Breakdance Contest
   begins 4:00
   lasts _____ hours
   ends 8:00

5. Band Practice
   begins 2:30
   lasts 1 hour,
   30 minutes
   ends ___:___

6. Play
   begins ___:___
   lasts 2 hours,
   30 minutes
   ends 8:30

7. Car Wash
   begins 9:00
   lasts _____ hours,
   _____ minutes
   ends 11:30

8. Dance Recital
   begins 4:30
   lasts _____ hours,
   _____ minutes
   ends 7:00

Basic Math Skills 3

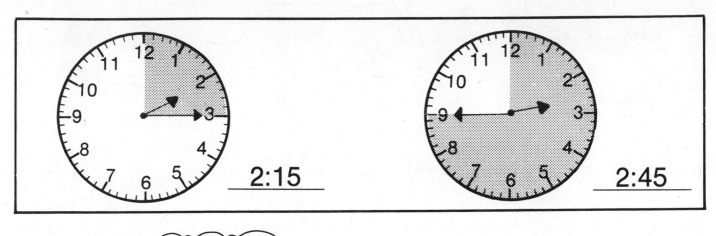

2:15

2:45

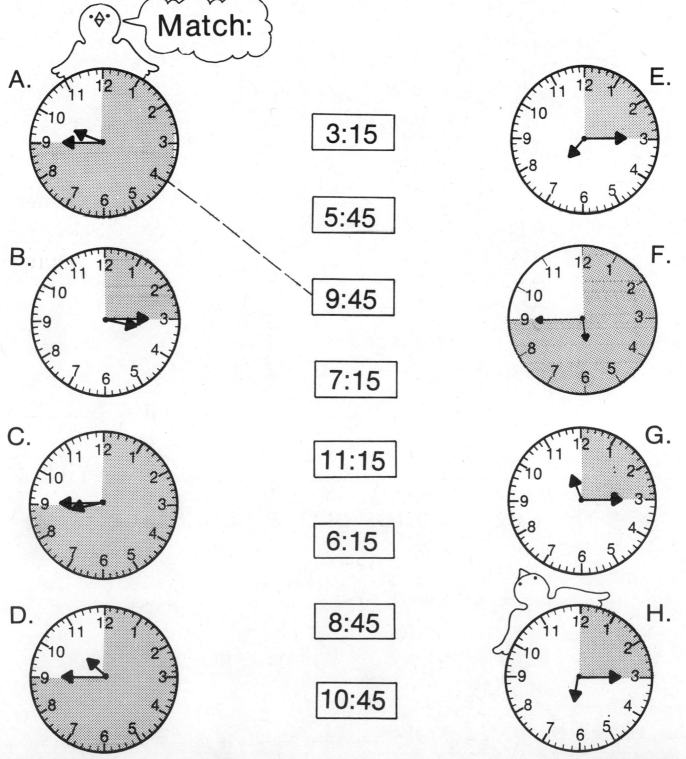

Match:

A.

3:15

5:45

9:45

7:15

B.

C.

11:15

6:15

D.

8:45

10:45

E.

F.

G.

H.

Basic Math Skills 3

Put the **minute hand** on the clock face.

3:45

7:15

3:15

7:45

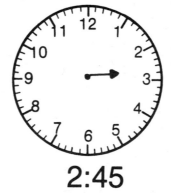

5:15

12:45

9:15

2:45

1:45

Put **both hands** on the clock face.

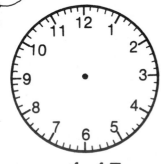

4:45

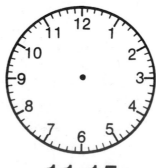

11:15

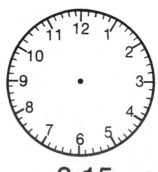

8:15

Basic Math Skills 3

What time is it?

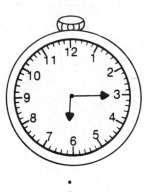

2:15

15 mins. after 2

___ : ___

___ mins. after ___

___ : ___

___ mins. after ___

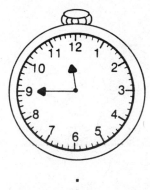
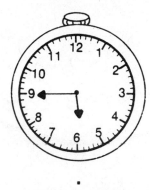
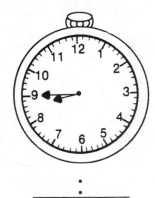

___ : ___

___ mins. until ___

___ : ___

___ mins. until ___

___ : ___

___ mins. until ___

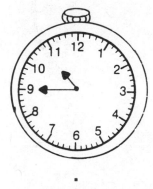

___ : ___

___ : ___

___ : ___

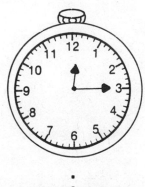

___ : ___

___ : ___

___ : ___

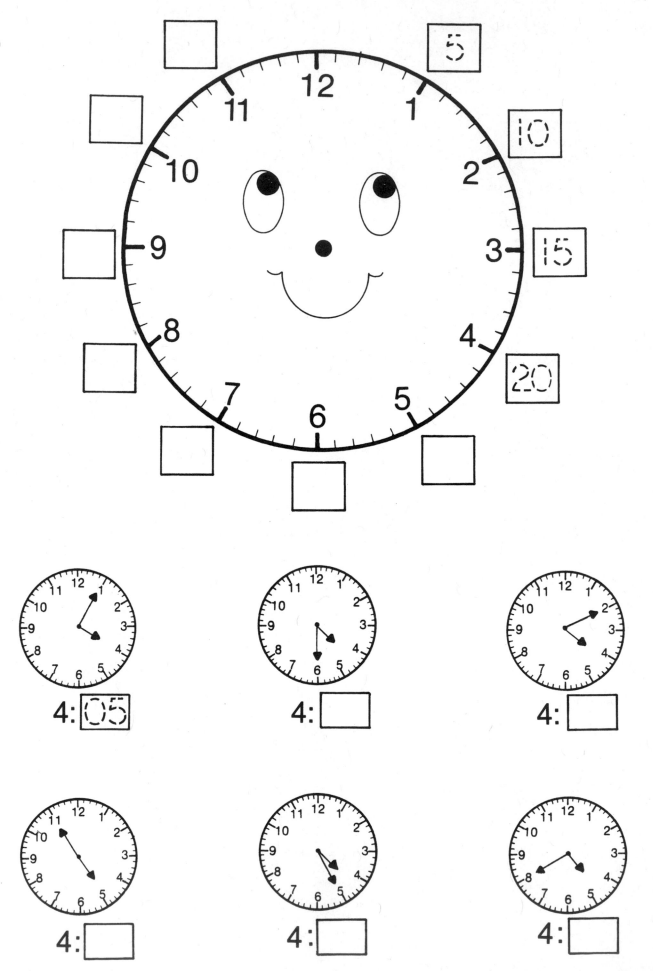

4 : **05**

4 : ☐

4 : ☐

4 : ☐

4 : ☐

4 : ☐

Basic Math Skills 3

Match:

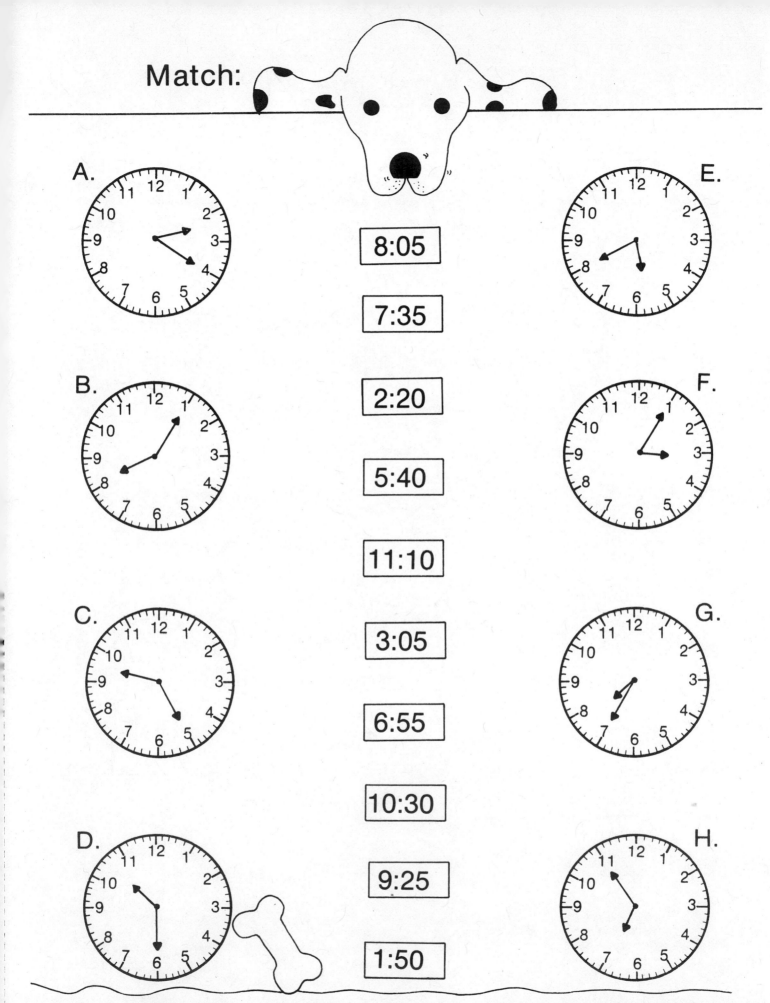

A.

E.

8:05

7:35

B.

F.

2:20

5:40

11:10

C.

G.

3:05

6:55

10:30

D.

H.

9:25

1:50

Basic Math Skills 3

What time is it?

5:10

___ : ___

___ : ___

___ : ___

___ : ___

___ : ___

___ : ___

___ : ___

___ : ___

___ : ___

___ : ___

Basic Math Skills 3

Put the **minute hand** on the clock face.

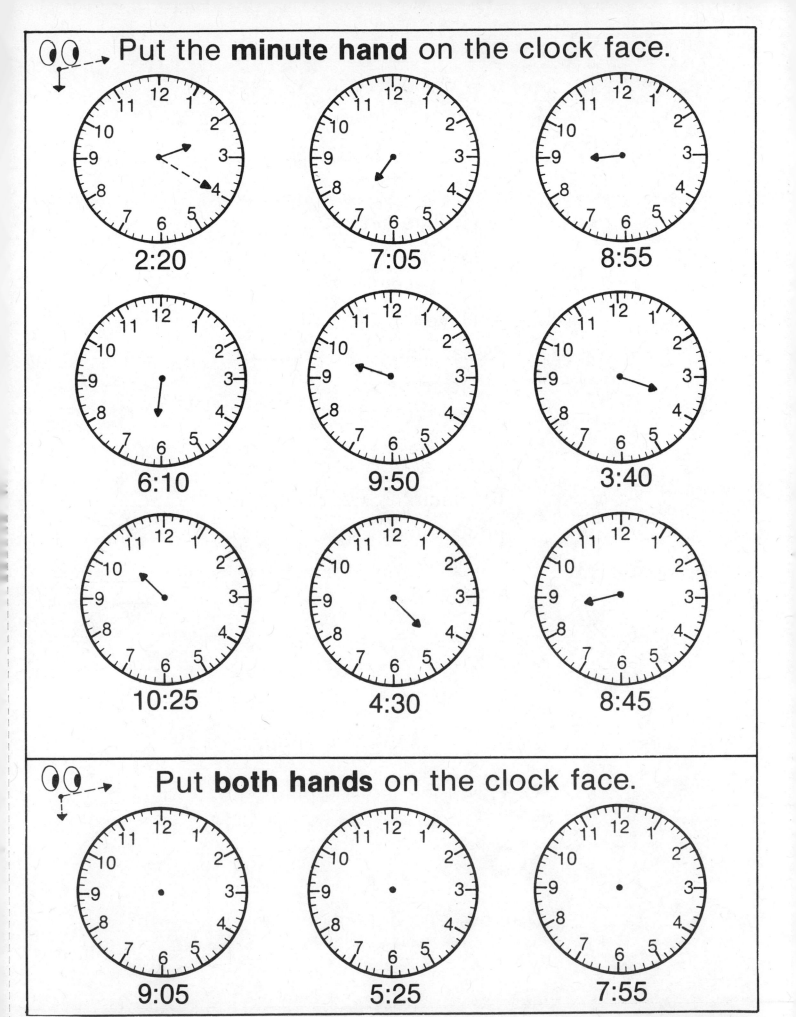

2:20

7:05

8:55

6:10

9:50

3:40

10:25

4:30

8:45

Put **both hands** on the clock face.

9:05

5:25

7:55

Basic Math Skills 3

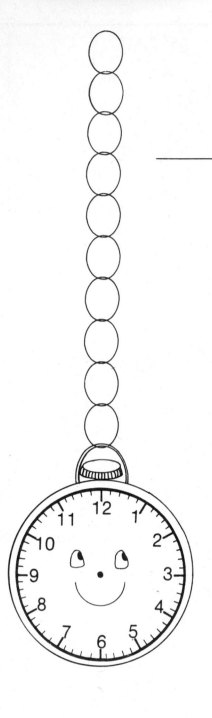

_____'s Saturday Schedule

A. What time did you . . .

1. Get up?   _____:_____
2. Eat breakfast?   _____:_____
3. Have lunch?   _____:_____
4. Eat dinner?   _____:_____
5. Go to bed?   _____:_____

B. Tell what you were doing at . . .

10:00 a.m. _____

11:30 a.m. _____

1:15 p.m. _____

3:45 p.m. _____

5:00 p.m. _____

7:30 p.m. _____

11:30 p.m. _____

C. How long did you play on Saturday?

about _____ hours _____ minutes

D. How long did you watch TV?

about _____ hours _____ minutes

A. 9:35

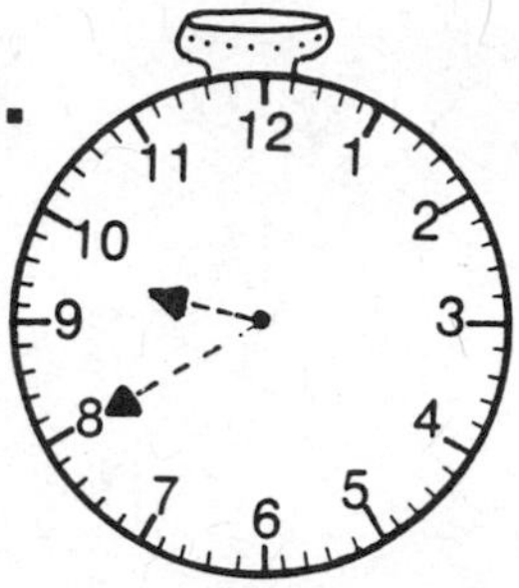

5 minutes later

B. 9:40

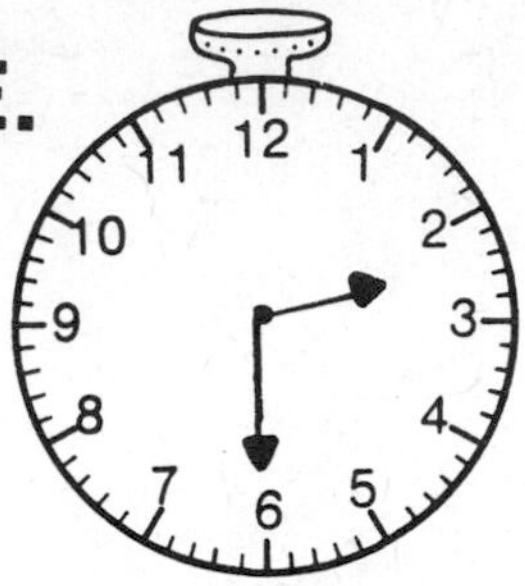

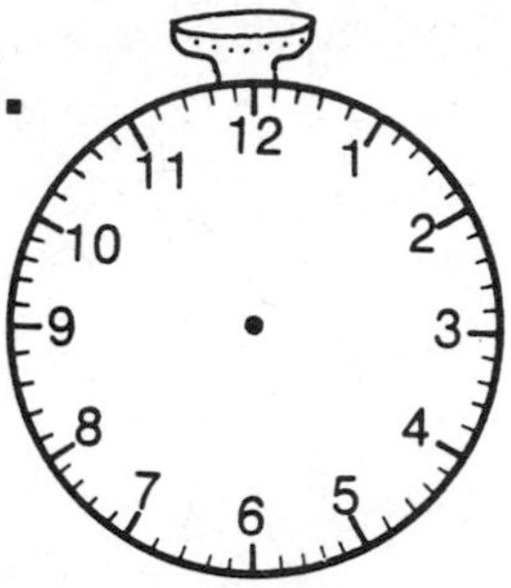

C. ___:___

10 minutes later

D. ___:___

E. ___:___

20 minutes later

F. ___:___

G. ___:___

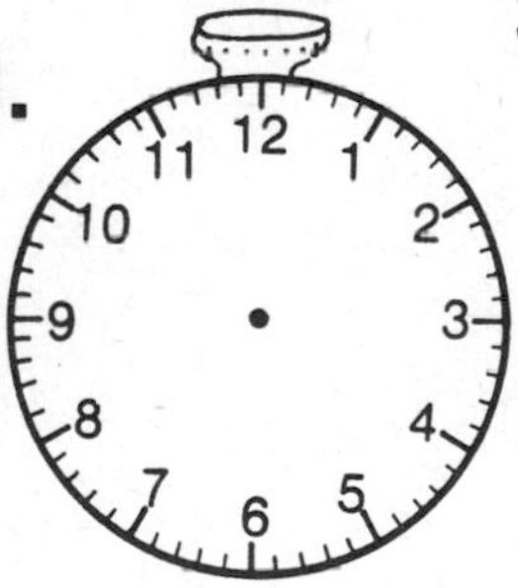

35 minutes later

H. ___:___

5 minutes later	15 minutes later
I. 4:20 ___:___	**M.** 4:40 ___:___
J. 6:15 ___:___	**N.** 6:05 ___:___
K. 10:25 ___:___	**O.** 10:25 ___:___
L. 2:40 ___:___	**P.** 1:30 ___:___

Count the minutes.

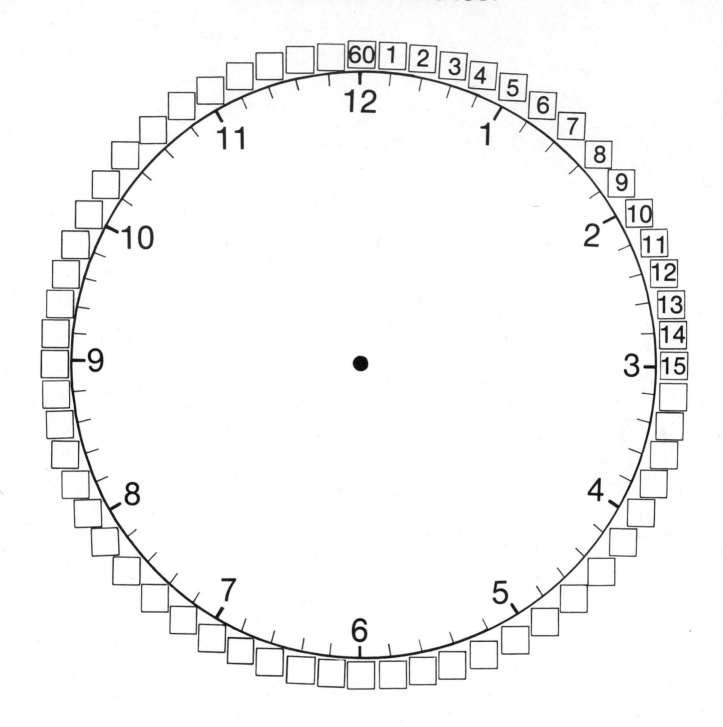

How many minutes are in one hour? ☐

How many minutes are in a half hour? ☐

Basic Math Skills 3

How many minutes?

A.

B.

C.

D.

E.

F.

G.

H.

I.

Match:

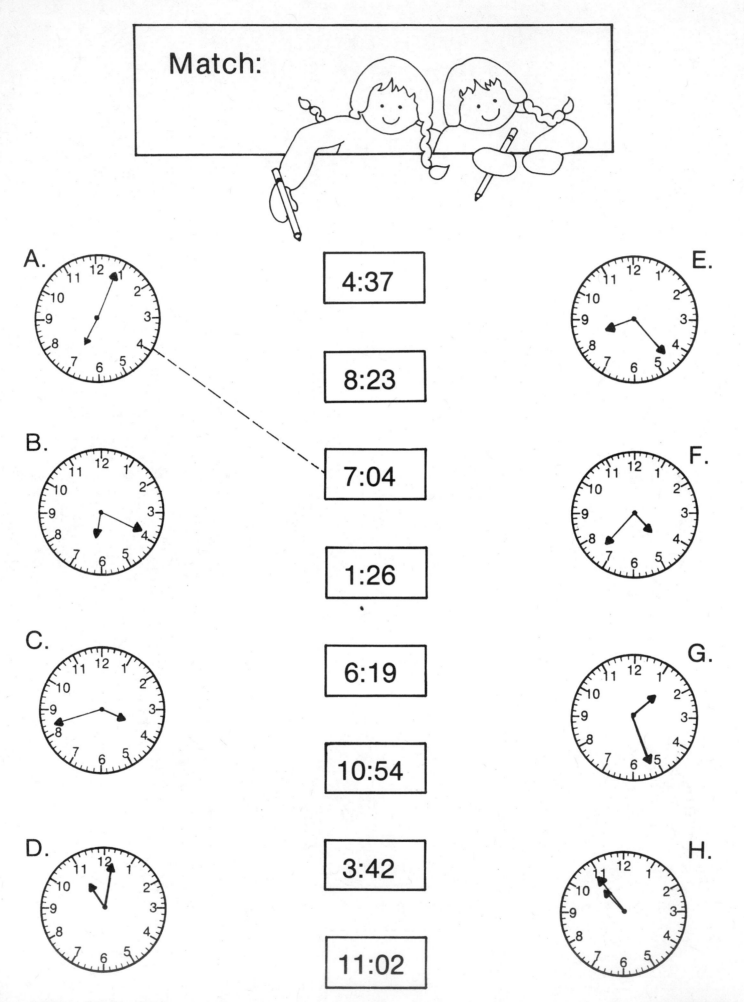

A.

E.

4:37

8:23

7:04

B.

F.

1:26

C.

6:19

G.

10:54

D.

3:42

H.

11:02

Basic Math Skills 3

Count the minutes.

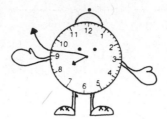

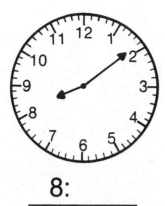

8: _____

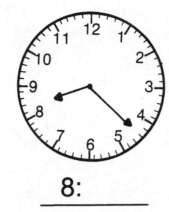

8: _____

8: _____

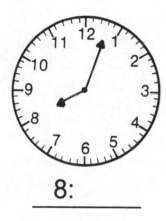

8: _____

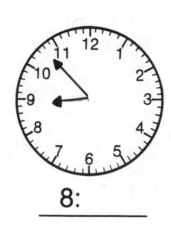

8: _____

8: _____

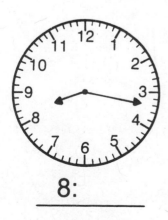

8: _____

8: _____

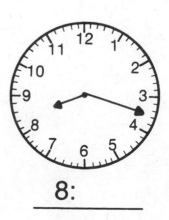

8: _____

Basic Math Skills 3

What time is it?

4:28

:

:

:

:

:

:

:

:

:

:

:

:

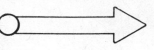
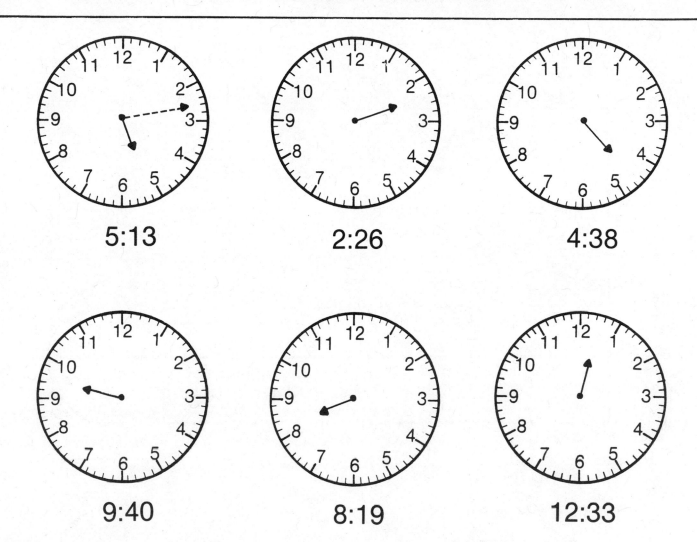

5:13   2:26   4:38

9:40   8:19   12:33

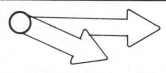 Put **both hands** on the clock face.

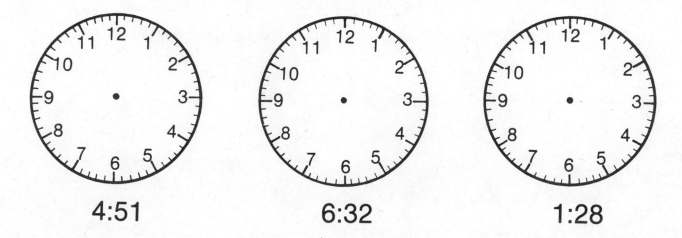

4:51   6:32   1:28

Basic Math Skills 3

Time To Relax!

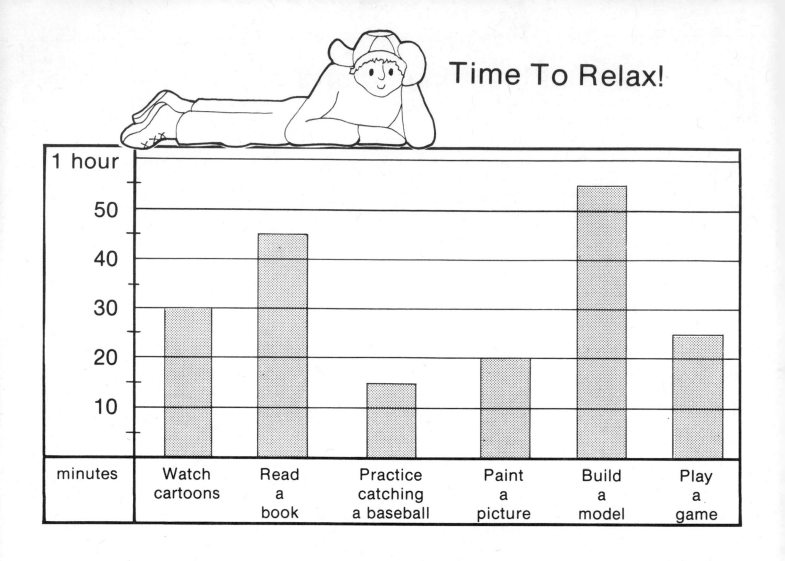

minutes	Watch cartoons	Read a book	Practice catching a baseball	Paint a picture	Build a model	Play a game

1. How many minutes did it take to . . .

    paint a picture? _____

    read a book? _____

    build a model? _____

2. Which activity takes the most time? _____

    Which activity takes the least time? _____

3. If we start playing a game at 6:15, what time will we finish? ____:____

4. The cartoon show stopped at 7:00.

    What time did it begin? ____:____

5. You have two hours until bedtime. Which three activities would you choose to do?

    _____, _____, _____

6. How long would it take you? ____ hours ____ minutes

                   Basic Math Skills 3

Timothy had a busy Saturday afternoon. Help him figure out his time schedule.

Activity	Started	Finished	Time spent:
1. Returned library books	12:00	12:25	____ minutes
2. Cut Mrs. Hartley's lawn	1:10	1:55	____ minutes
3. Fixed a snack and ate it.	2:18	2:28	____ minutes
4. Changed a flat tire on his bike	2:35	____:____	23 minutes
5. Played catch with his friends at the park	3:15	4:05	____ minutes
6. Listened to a new record album	4:15	____:____	43 minutes
7. Practiced the piano	____:____	6:10	1 hour
8. Set the dinner table for mom	6:18	____:____	10 minutes
9. Watched T.V.	8:00	____:____	1 hour, 30 minutes

Basic Math Skills 3

A.M or P.M.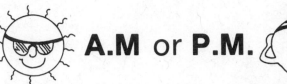

A.M. is used for time after 12:00 midnight and before 12:00 noon.

P.M. is used for times after 12:00 noon and before 12:00 midnight.

1. wake up and turn off the alarm   A.M.

2. have a snack before you play   _____

3. help wash the dinner dishes   _____

4. get out of bed   _____

5. turn off the lights and go to sleep   _____

6. dress for school   _____

7. go to bed   _____

8. do your homework after school   _____

9. say good-morning to your teacher   _____

10. eat a good breakfast   _____

11. put on your pajamas   _____

12. walk to school (Don't be late!)   _____

Dr. Jones' Appointment Schedule

Pet	Appointment
Bubbles	9:15
Clifton	10:00
Tweeter	____ : ____
Muffin	1:30
Speedy	____ : ____
Patches	____ : ____

1. Write these appointments on Dr. Jones' schedules.

   Tweeter — 45 minutes after Clifton's appointment
   Patches — 1 hour and 30 minutes after Muffin's appointment
   Speedy — 30 minutes before Patches' appointment

2. Dr. Jones opened her office at 8:30. How long did she have to get ready for her first appointment:

   ____ mins.

3. Bubbles didn't want her shots. She wiggled so much it took Dr. Jones 20 minutes. What time did she finish?

   ____ : ____

4. Dr. Jones finished with Patches at 3:30. She had an operation that lasted 1 hour and 15 minutes. What time did she finish for the day? _____

5. How long did Dr. Jones work? (Remember, she started at 8:30.)

   ____ hours ____ minutes

Think About It

*Be careful. Some of these questions are tricky!

1. Luiz can eat 1 slice of pizza in 3 minutes. How long will it take him to eat 4 slices?

   _____

2. If Luiz started eating his pizza at 6:25, when would he finish eating the 4 slices?

   _____

3. Carol can bounce a ball 40 times in one minute. How many times can she bounce the ball in 5 minutes?

   _____

4. If Carol starts bouncing her ball at 4:00, when would she finish 120 bounces?

   _____

5. Alex likes to make paper airplanes. He can make one airplane in 7 minutes. How many airplanes can he make in 42 minutes?

   _____

6. If Alex starts at 3:10, what time will he finish 3 airplanes?

   _____

7. Joan can bake 1 dozen cookies in 12 minutes. How long will it take to bake 3 dozen cookies?

   _____

8. If Joan started at 1:15, when would she finish baking the 3 dozen cookies?

   _____

Changing   Times

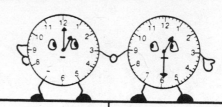

1.

 $\underline{11:30}$

1 hour 30 minutes
later

2.

 $\underline{\quad:\quad}$

50 minutes
later

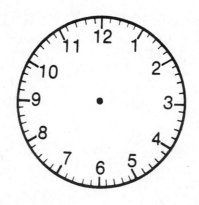

3.

 $\underline{\quad:\quad}$

1 hour 12 minutes
later

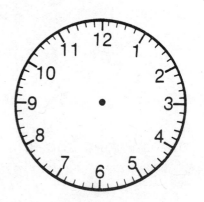

4.

 $\underline{\quad:\quad}$

35 minutes
earlier

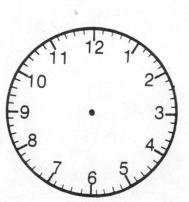

5.

 $\underline{\quad:\quad}$

2 hours 30 minutes
earlier

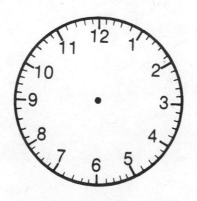

6.

 $\underline{\quad:\quad}$

1 hour 45 minutes
earlier

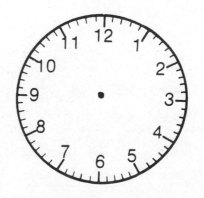

Basic Math Skills 3

Homework — **Just One Minute!**

A. Can you do it in one minute?

1. Count to 100 _____
2. Put on your shoes and tie the laces _____
3. Make a peanut butter sandwich _____
4. Put on a jacket and button it up _____
5. Write the alphabet _____

B. How many times can you _____ in one minute?

1. Touch your toes _____ times
2. Bounce a ball _____ times
3. Run around your house _____ times
   (Outside, of course!)
4. Hop on one foot _____ times
5. Write your **whole** name _____ times

Who timed you? _____

How? _____

Basic Math Skills 3

60 seconds = 1 minute

60 minutes = 1 hour

24 hours = 1 day

7 days = 1 week

52 weeks = 1 year

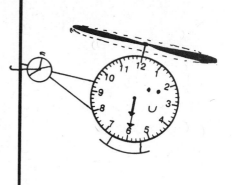

1. 120 seconds = _____ minutes

    _____ seconds = 5 minutes

    240 seconds = _____ minutes

2. 180 minutes = _____ hours

    _____ minutes = 4 hours

    30 minutes = _____ hour

3. 48 hours = _____ days

    _____ hours = 3 days

    _____ hours = 5 days

4. 21 days = _____ weeks

    _____ days = 9 weeks

    35 days = _____ weeks

5. 104 weeks = _____ years

    _____ weeks = 3 years

    _____ weeks = 5 years

6. How many weeks
    in 10 years?

    _____ weeks

 Bonus!

How many hours in a week?

_____ hours

 Super Bonus!!!

How many minutes in a week?

_____ minutes

 Earlier Later

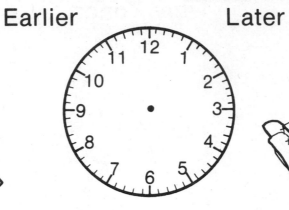

1 hour earlier		1 hour later		30 minutes earlier		30 minutes later
3:00	4:00	5:00		5:30	6:00	6:30
___:___	8:30	___:___		___:___	12:30	___:___
___:___	11:15	___:___		___:___	9:45	___:___
___:___	2:06	___:___		___:___	7:25	___:___
___:___	3:58	___:___		___:___	10:15	___:___

2 hours earlier		2 hours later		10 minutes earlier		10 minutes later
7:00	9:00	11:00		7:00	7:10	7:20
___:___	6:10	___:___		___:___	9:40	___:___
___:___	4:37	___:___		___:___	11:25	___:___
___:___	2:30	___:___		___:___	3:30	___:___
___:___	11:00	___:___		___:___	5:15	___:___

Time Zones

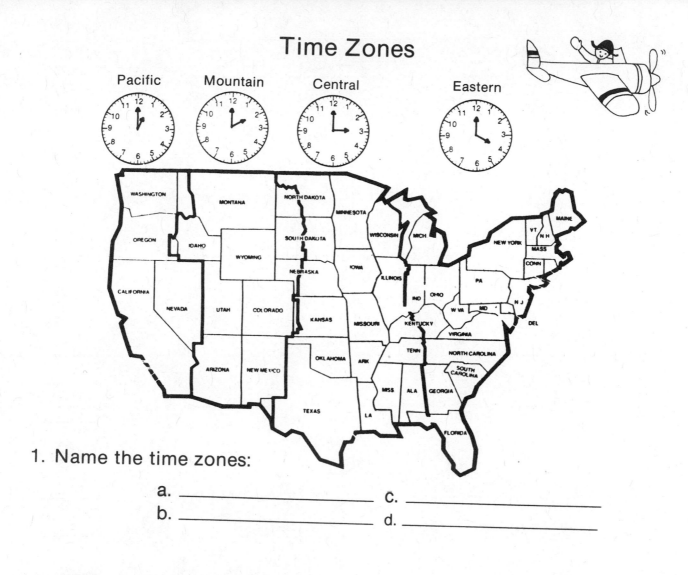

Pacific   Mountain   Central   Eastern

1. Name the time zones:

   a. _____   c. _____
   b. _____   d. _____

2. If it is 1:00 in California, it will be:

   _____:_____ in Utah   _____:_____ in Missouri
   _____:_____ in Florida   _____:_____ in Oregon
   _____:_____ in Iowa   _____:_____ in Maine

3. Harry lives in New Mexico. He called his grandmother in Oklahoma. If he called at 2:15, what time was it at his grandmother's? _____:_____

4. How many hours difference is there between each time zone? _____

   Super Bonus:
   Allen left California at 1:00. It took 7 hours to fly to New York. What time did he arrive? _____

          Basic Math Skills 3

Time Test

A. What time is it?

1.
___ : ___

2.
___ : ___

3.
___ : ___

4.
___ : ___

5.
___ : ___

6.
___ : ___

7.
___ : ___

8.
___ : ___

B. Put the hands on the clock face.

1.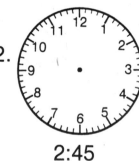
8:30

2.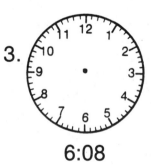
2:45

3.
6:08

4. 10:19

C. A.M. or P.M.

1. Eat dinner _____   2. Go to bed _____

3. Leave for school _____   4. Finish breakfast _____

D. How many . . .

1. minutes in an hour?   _____ minutes

2. hours in a day?   _____ hours

3. days in a week?   _____ days

4. weeks in a year?   _____ weeks

         Basic Math Skills 3

This

Time Award

goes to

_____
name

for a job well done.

NOTE: Use these blank clocks to create
additional practice pages of your own.

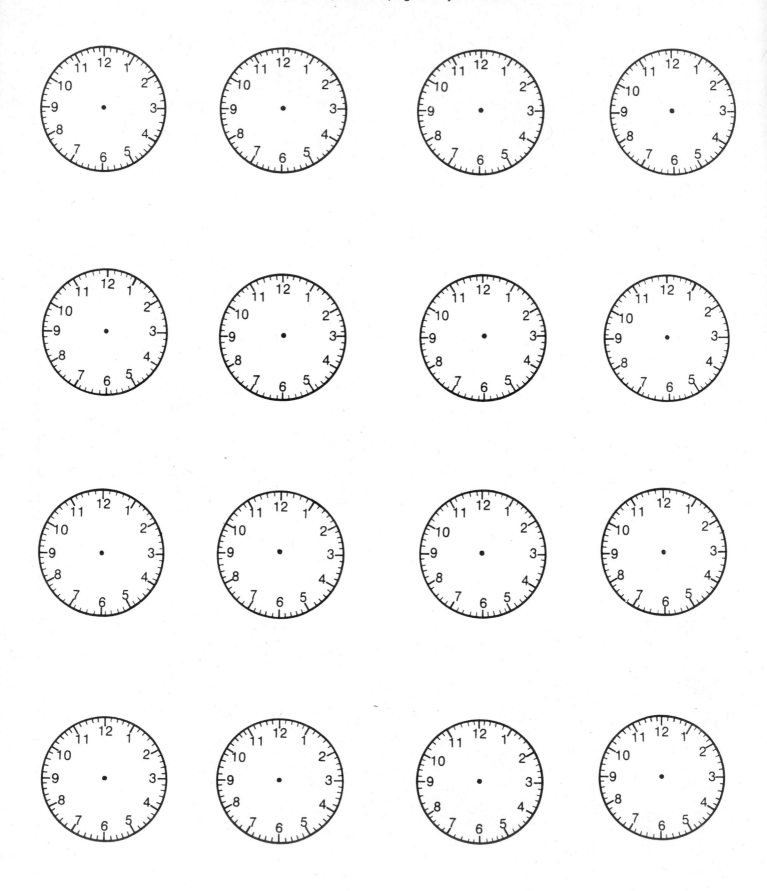

Practice
Money Skills

Value and Recognition
of Coins and Bills

This section contains a variety of activities designed to
motivate students to practice money skills.

- *Recognition and value of coins and bills*

- *Counting sets of money*

- *Greater than, less than, equal to*

- *Making change*

- *Sums and differences*

- *Word problems*

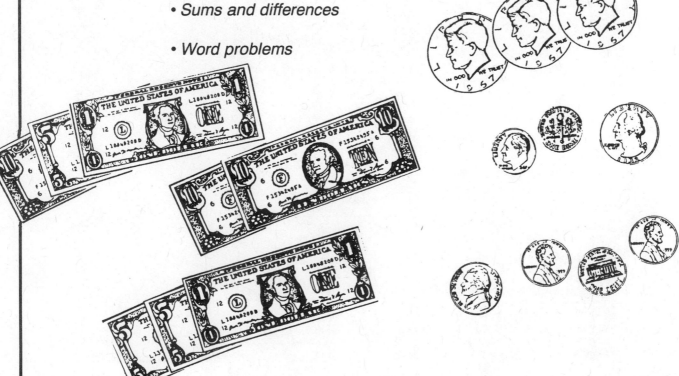

Answer Key

Page 105: Answers will vary.

Page 106:
1. >	2. >	3. >	4. =	5. <	6. <	7. >	8. =
9. <	10. >	11. >	12. <	13. >	14. <	15. >	16. =

Page 107:

Page 108:
1. $ .50 $1.00   2. $ .25 $ .50 $ .75 $ 1.00
3. $ .10 $ .20 $ .30 $ .40 $ .50
   $ .60 $ .70 $ .80 $ .90 $1.00
4. $ .05 $ .10 $ .15 $ .20 $ .25
   $ .30 $ .35 $ .40 $ .45 $ .50
   $ .55 $ .60 $ .65 $ .70 $ .75
   $ .80 $ .85 $ .90 $ .95 $1.00

Page 109: Answers will vary.

Page 110: 1. 15¢ 2. 21¢ 3. 18¢ 4. 10¢ 5. 7¢ 6. 17¢

Page 111: 1. 50¢ 2. 7¢ 3. 42¢ 4. 98¢ 5. 20¢ 6. 99¢ coins will vary.

Page 112: 1. 26¢ 2. 45¢ 3. 33¢ 4. 75¢ 5. 72¢ 6. 83¢ 7. 85¢ 8. 95¢
  9. 2n 2d   1hd, 1q   1q, 1d   2hd   1q, 1n

Page 113: 1. $1.93 2. $3.10 3. $4.67 4. $4.86 5. $2.75 6. $1.09 7. $5.41 8. $2.22 9. $1.20 10. $3.00
  11. $1.50 12. $1.45 13. $2.05 14. $1.75

Page 114: 1. Yes 2. No 3. Yes 4. Yes 5. No

Page 115: 1. $ .33 2. $ .05 3. $ .75 4. $ .50 5. .40   6. robot 7. bear 8. bear and plane

Page 116: 1. $1.96 2. $1.50 3. $2.00 4. $2.75 5. $4.50 6. $2.00 7. $5.30 8. $10.00

Page 117: Answers will vary.

Page 118: rocket ship

Page 119: He will quack up.

Page 120:

Page 121: 1. $3.87 2. $9.00 3. $1.30 4. $5.01 5. $2.72 $6.87 $4.13 $9.92 $3.90

Page 122: 1. soccer ball   2. baseball   3. bowling ball   4. football   5. $2.05   6. $2.50
     or baseball   or less expen-
                        sive balls

Page 123: 1. 1q, 1d, 1p   2. 2q, 1p   3. 1hd, 1q, 1p   4. 1hd, 1q, 1d,   5. 1$, 1d   6. 1$, 2hd, 2d
                                         1n, 1p

Page 124: 1. 34¢ 2. 50¢ 3. 6   4. 6   5. 25¢ 6. $1.00 7. Answers will vary.

Page 125: 1. 85¢ 2. 55¢ 3. 25¢ 4. $5.00 5. 40¢ 6. $1.76 7. $1.13 8. $4.50

Page 126: 1. $1.00 $ .10   2. Answers will vary. $ .20   3. $2.00 $ .50
    4. $2.35 $ .07   5. $5.10 $ .02

Page 127: 1. $3.00 $2.00   2. $3.00 $2.00   3. $8.00 $2.00
    4. $2.94 $ .06   5. $8.75 $1.25   6. $16.00 $4.00

Page 128: 1. $1.25 2. $1.22 3. $1.99 4. $2.74 5. Answers will vary.

Page 129: 1. $2.45 2. $2.70 3. $2.35 4. $3.45 5. Answers will vary.   6. Answers will vary.

Page 130: 1. $42.77 $80.03 $87.69 $81.09
    2. $27.25 $11.01 $19.08 $10.05
    3. $ .25   4. $3.50 5. $56.00   6. $6.00   7. $9.10

Page 131: 1. $12.85   2. $10.90   3. $11.50   4. $17.50   5. $11.45   6. $20.08
    7. Janice   8. Olive

Page 132: 1. $ .72   2. $1.00   3. 13   4. $1.70   5. $1.16   6. 51
    7. 40   8. $4.80

Page 133: 1. $2.00   2. $2.85   3. $4.10   4. $1.30   5. Answers will vary
    6. Answers will vary.

Page 134: 2. $1.80 school supplies $6.53 present $1.80 ice cream   15¢ lost
    3. $23.13   4. $21.84   5. $1.29

Page 135: a. $1.20   b. $1.00   c. $3.50   d. $21.00

Page 136: 1. $14.00   2. $4.00   3. $9.60   4. $68.00   5. $12.00   6. $22.40
    $7.00 $1.00 $3.20 $34.00 $ 4.00 $11.20
    $7.00 $3.00 $6.40 $34.00 $8.00 $11.20
    Super Bonus: $71.10

Basic Math Skills 3

quarter	dime	nickel	penny

25¢	10¢	5¢	1¢

Money Magnet Club

$

Name

Circle coins to make these sums:

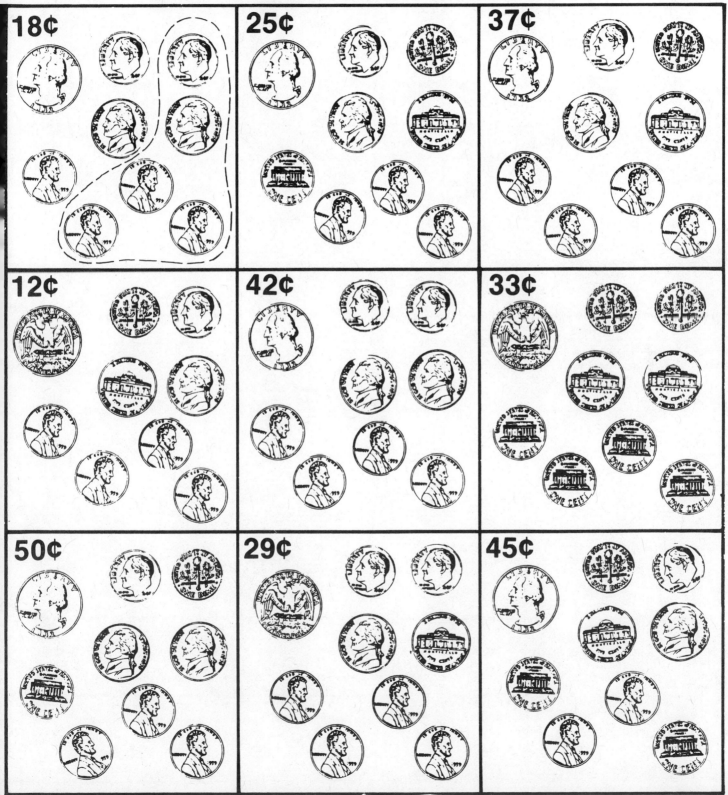

18¢   **25¢**   **37¢**

12¢   **42¢**   **33¢**

50¢   **29¢**   **45¢**

Basic Math Skills 3

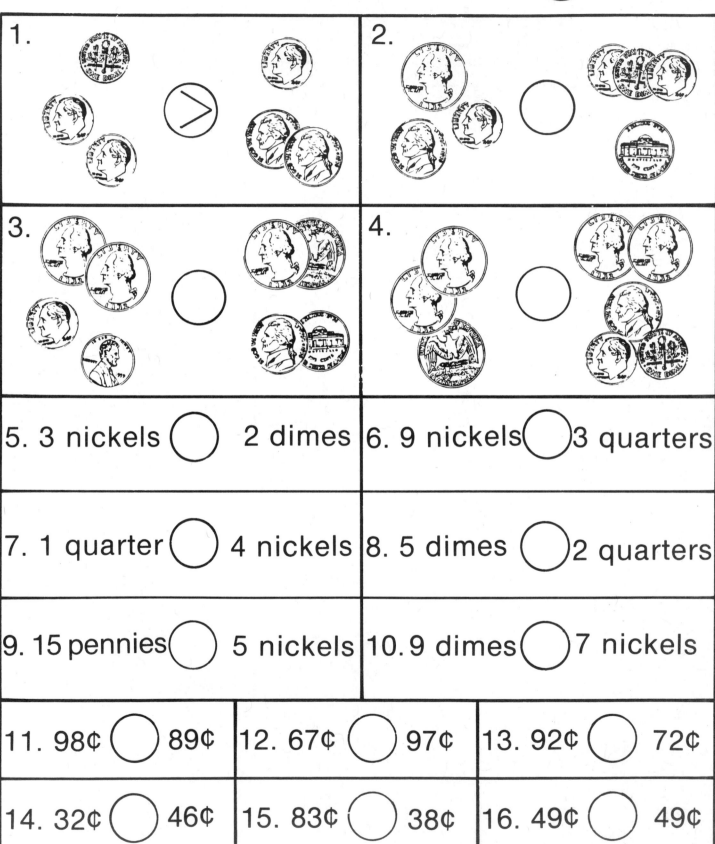

1.

2.

3.

4.

5. 3 nickels ◯ 2 dimes

6. 9 nickels ◯ 3 quarters

7. 1 quarter ◯ 4 nickels

8. 5 dimes ◯ 2 quarters

9. 15 pennies ◯ 5 nickels

10. 9 dimes ◯ 7 nickels

11. 98¢ ◯ 89¢

12. 67¢ ◯ 97¢

13. 92¢ ◯ 72¢

14. 32¢ ◯ 46¢

15. 83¢ ◯ 38¢

16. 49¢ ◯ 49¢

Basic Math Skills 3

half dollar   50 cents   50¢

Color sets of 25¢ yellow.
Color sets of 50¢ red.

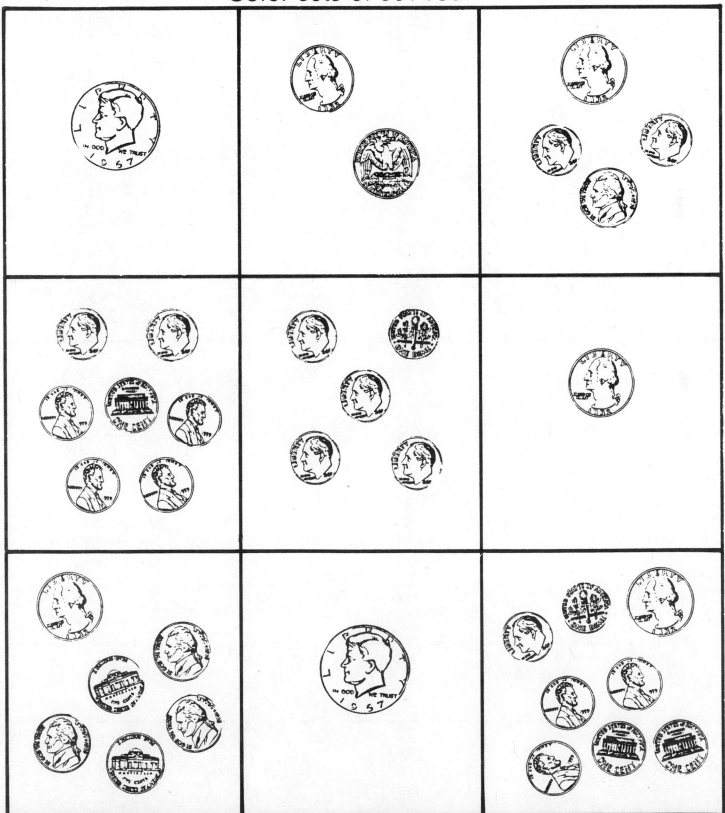

Count to $1.00.

1.  $ __50__ $ __100__   2. $ __.25__ $ __.__ $ __.__ $ __.__

3. $ __.10__ $ __.__ $ __.__ $ __.__ $ __.__

   $ __.__ $ __.__ $ __.__ $ __.__ $ __.__

4. $ __.05__ $ __.10__ $ __.__ $ __.__ $ __.__

   $ __.__ $ __.__ $ __.__ $ __.__ $ __.__

   $ __.__ $ __.__ $ __.__ $ __.__ $ __.__

   $ __.__ $ __.__ $ __.__ $ __.__ $ __.__

5. How many in $1.00? _____

   How many in $1.00? _____

   How many in $1.00? _____

   How many in $1.00? _____

   How many in $1.00? _____

Basic Math Skills 3

Circle coins to make sets of $1.00.

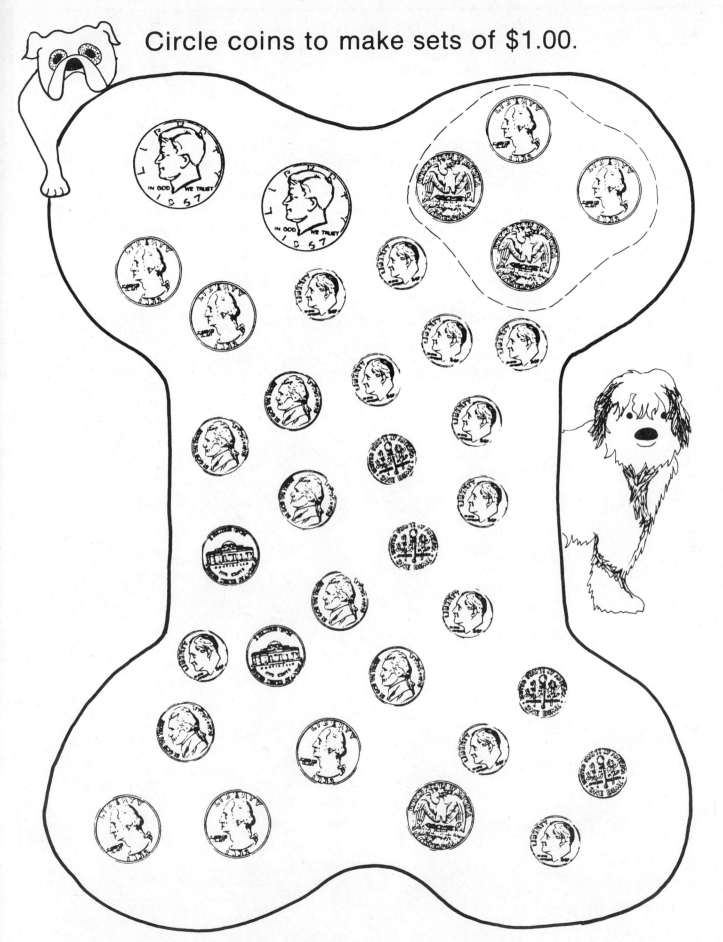

How many sets of $1.00 did you find? _____

Basic Math Skills 3

MAKING CHANGE

Cost:	You have:	Change:
1. 45¢		15¢
2. 53¢		
3. 26¢		
4. 89¢		
5. 71¢		
6. 90¢		

Basic Math Skills 3

THINK ABOUT IT

1. Teddy had 20¢.
   He got 30¢.
   He has _____¢ in all.

2. Jay had 35¢.
   He spent 28¢.
   He has _____¢ left.

3. Christy had 87¢
   She spent 45¢.
   She has _____¢ left.

4. Henry had 28¢.
   He earned 45¢.
   He found 25¢.
   He has _____¢ in all.

5. Suzanne had 75¢.
   She spent 24¢.
   Then she spent 31¢.
   She has _____¢ left.

6. Ralph had 34¢.
   He got 25¢ from his mom
   and 40¢ from his dad.
   He has _____¢ in all.

Put an X on the amount of money the children need.

Basic Math Skills 3

Money Magnet Club

$

Name _____

MATCH:

1. two dimes, six pennies

2. one quarter, four nickels

3. five nickels, eight pennies

4. three quarters

5. six dimes, twelve pennies

6. two quarters, three dimes, three pennies

7. one half dollar, one quarter, one dime

8. one half dollar, four dimes, one nickel

9. How can you make it with 2 coins?

75¢

26¢

85¢

83¢

45¢

72¢

33¢

95¢

10¢ _____   20¢_____   75¢_____

35¢_____ $1.00_____   30¢_____

1. 193¢ = <u>$1.93</u>

2. 310¢ = _____

3. 467¢ = _____

4. 486¢ = _____

5. 275¢ = _____

6. 109¢ = _____

7. 541¢ = _____

8. 222¢ = _____

9.

$ _____ . _____

10.

$ _____ . _____

11.

$ _____ . _____

12.

$ _____ . _____

13.

$ _____ . _____

14.

$ _____ . _____

CAN YOU BUY IT?

Costs:	You have:	Yes	No

1.  $2.92

2. $1.59

3. $2.48

4. 5 $10.50

5. $7.15

Basic Math Skills 3

HOW MUCH DO YOU HAVE LEFT?

Had:	Bought:	Had left:

1.  $1.34

$$\begin{array}{r} 1.67 \\ -1.34 \end{array}$$

$ _____ . _____

2.  $2.95

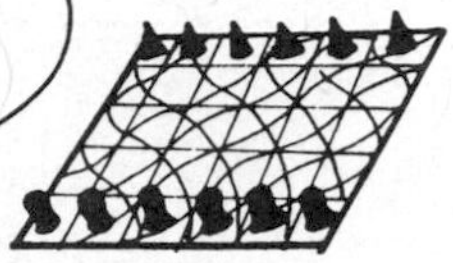

$ _____ . _____

3.  $4.75

$ _____ . _____

4.  $5.25

$ _____ . _____

5.  $3.10

$ _____ . _____

6. What costs the least? _____

7. What costs the most? _____

8. Which two toys could you buy for $10.00?

_____ and _____

Basic Math Skills 3

HOW MUCH DO YOU SEE?

1.  $1.96

2.  _____

3.  _____

4.  _____

5.  _____

6.  _____

7.  _____

8. _____

X the largest amount.   Circle the smallest amount.

116   Basic Math Skills 3

The Sticker Store

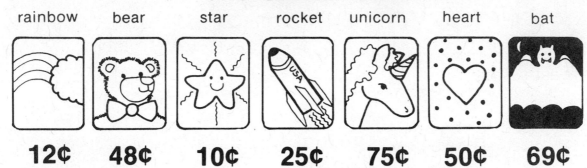

rainbow	bear	star	rocket	unicorn	heart	bat
12¢	48¢	10¢	25¢	75¢	50¢	69¢

1. Diane has 25¢.
   What stickers
   can she buy?

   Was there any money
   left? _____

2. Bernard has 50¢.
   What stickers
   can he buy?

   Was there any money
   left? _____

3. Sally has 75¢.
   What stickers
   can she buy?

   Was there any money
   left? _____

4. Jerome has 95¢
   What stickers
   can he buy?

   Was there any money
   left? _____

If you had $1.00, what
stickers would you
buy?

_____

_____

_____

1. Write the amount in each box.
2. Connect the dots. Always go to the next largest sum.

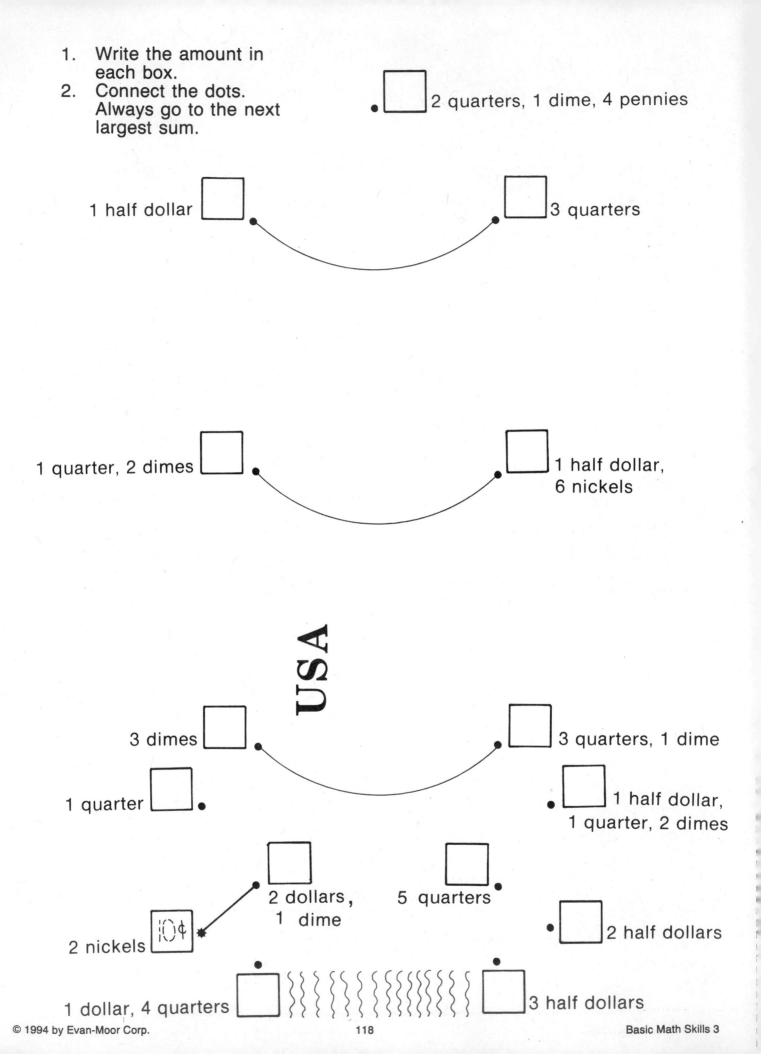

2 quarters, 1 dime, 4 pennies

1 half dollar

3 quarters

1 quarter, 2 dimes

1 half dollar, 6 nickels

USA

3 dimes

3 quarters, 1 dime

1 quarter

1 half dollar, 1 quarter, 2 dimes

2 dollars, 1 dime

5 quarters

2 nickels   10¢

2 half dollars

1 dollar, 4 quarters

3 half dollars

Basic Math Skills 3

Why can't a duck fly upside down?

| $ .18 **H** |
| $ .32 **I** |
| $ .36 **L** |
| $ .45 **C** |

| $ .50 **A** |
| $ .75 **E** |
| $ .96 **W** |

| $1.00 **P** |
| $1.40 **U** |
| $4.00 **K** |
| $8.00 **Q** |

3 🍬 6¢ each $ .18	3 🍭 25¢ each $. ___
⌐⌐	

2 🧊 48¢ each $ ___ . ___	8 ⌒ 4¢ each $ ___ . ___	4 🥢 9¢ each $ ___ . ___	6 🔴 6¢ each $ ___ . ___

4 YUM $2.00 each $ ___ . ___	70 ◎ 2¢ each $ ___ . ___	10 ▭ 5¢ each $ ___ . ___	5 🫘 9¢ each $ ___ . ___	4 ✉ $1.00 each $ ___ . ___

4 🍡 35¢ each $ ___ . ___	2 🍦 50¢ each $ ___ . ___

Basic Math Skills 3

Color $5 **yellow.**

Color more than $5 **red.**

Color less than $5 **black.**

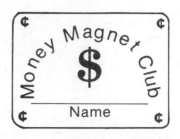

Money Magnet Club

$

Name

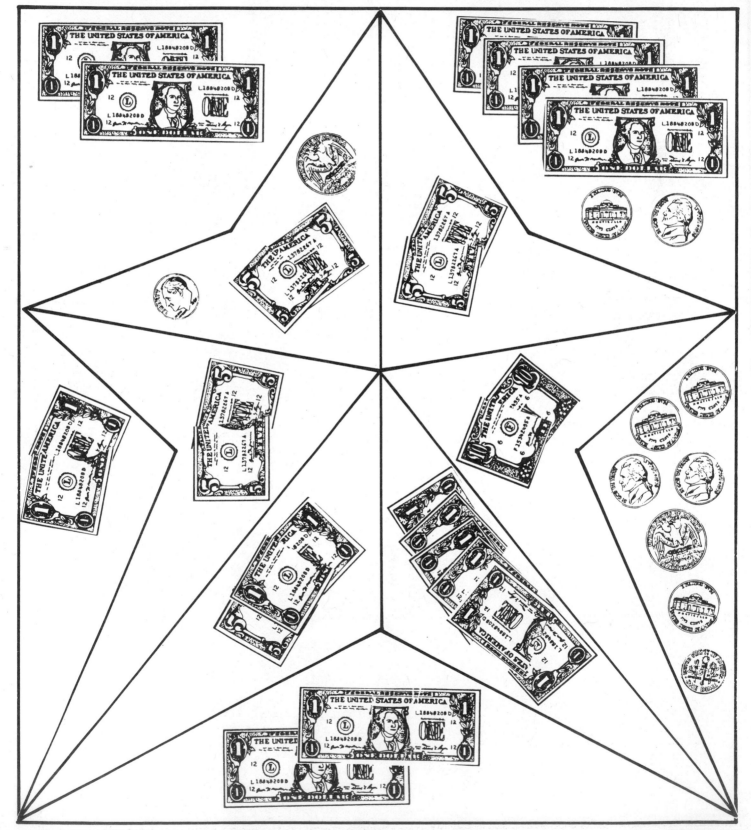

Basic Math Skills 3

SUMS AND DIFFERENCES

1.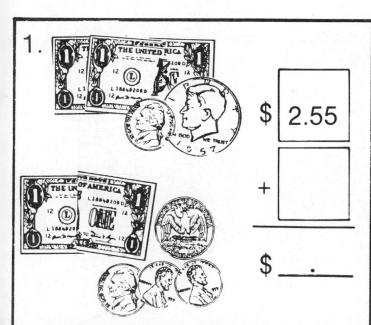

$ | 2.55
+ |
___
$ _____ . _____

2.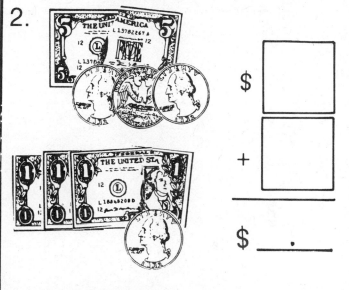

$ |
+ |
___
$ _____ . _____

3.

$ | 2.65
- | 1.35
___
$ _____ . _____

4.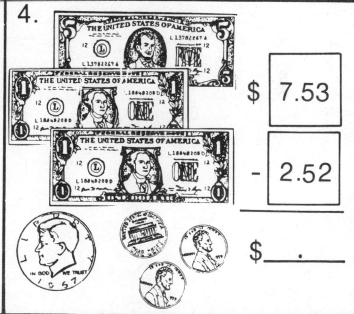

$ | 7.53
- | 2.52
___
$ _____ . _____

5.

$3.98	$2.61	$9.06	$8.64	$6.88
-1.26	+4.26	-4.93	+1.28	-2.98
$.	$.	$.	$.	$.

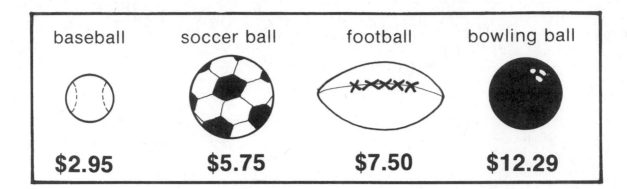

baseball	soccer ball	football	bowling ball
$2.95	$5.75	$7.50	$12.29

1. Albert has

What can he buy?

_____

2. Emily has

What can she buy?

_____

3. Ramona has

What can she buy?

_____

4. Damon has

What can he buy?

_____

5. I have $5.00.
   I buy a baseball.
   How much change do
   I get back? $ _____

6. I have $10.00.
   I buy a football.
   How much change do
   I get back?
   $ _____

WHAT IS IN MY POCKET?

1.

37¢

4 coins are
in my pocket. _2_

2.

51¢

3 coins are
in my pocket. ____

3.

76¢

3 coins are
in my pocket. ____

4.

91¢

5 coins are
in my pocket. ____

5.

$1.10

2 pieces of
money are in
my pocket. ____

6.

$2.20

5 pieces of
money are in
my pocket. ____

Basic Math Skills 3

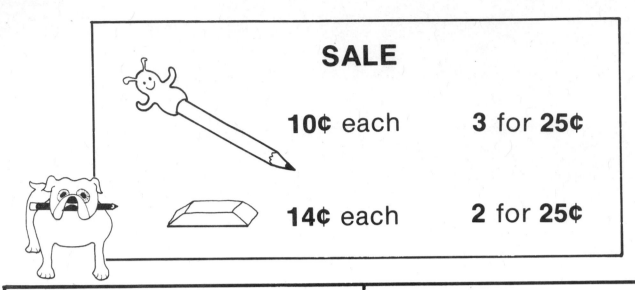

SALE

10¢ each   **3** for **25¢**

14¢ each   **2** for **25¢**

1. 1 eraser
   2 pencils
   Total cost _____
	2. 2 erasers
	   3 pencils
	   Total cost _____

3. Spent 50¢
   How many pencils? _____
	4. Spent 75¢
	   How many erasers? _____

5. 6 pencils
   2 erasers
   Change from $1.00? _____
	6. 1 dozen pencils
	   Total cost? _____

7. What can you buy for exactly 50¢?

Color the answers **red**:

1. 10¢ more than 3 quarters   _____

2. 4 dimes less than 95¢   _____

3. 9 nickels minus 2 dimes   _____

4. 38¢ more than $4.62   _____

5. 4 nickels times two   _____

6. $4.65 minus $2.89   _____

7. 63¢ plus a half dollar   _____

8. 3 dollars plus 6 quarters   _____

Color all other numbers blue.

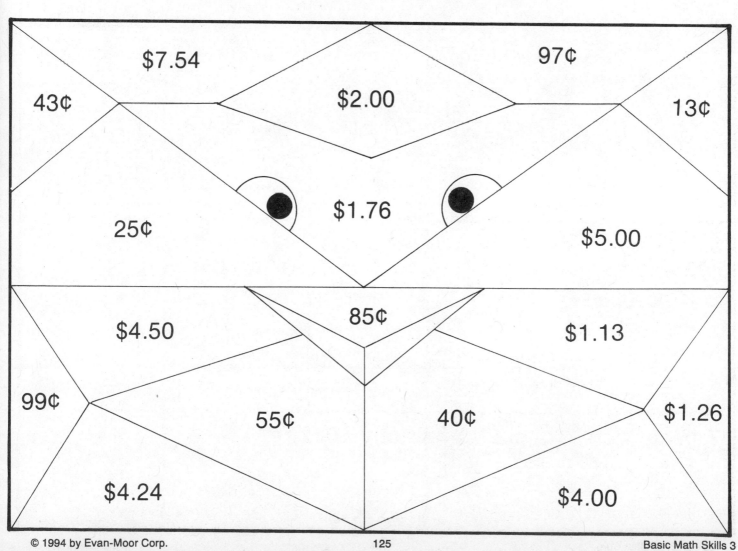

MAKING CHANGE

You have:	Cost:	Give clerk:	Change:
1.	$ .90	$ 1.00	$ .10
2.	$1.30	$ ___.___	$ ___.___
3.	$1.50	$ ___.___	$ ___.___
4.	$2.28	$ ___.___	$ ___.___
5.	$5.08	$ ___.___	$ ___.___

Basic Math Skills 3

SHOPPING FOR ROWDY

1.
$1.00 each

Carlos bought 3.

Cost $ 3.00

Change
from $5? $ 2.00

2.
$1.50

Carlos bought 2.

Cost $____.____

Change
from $5? $____.____

3.
$2.00 each

Carlos bought 4.

Cost $____.____

Change
from $10? $____.____

4.
$ .98 each

Carlos bought 3.

Cost $____.____

Change
from $3? $____.____

5.

$8.75 each

Carlos bought 1.

Cost $____.____

Change
from $10? $____.____

6.
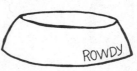
$8.00 each

Carlos bought 2.

Cost $____.____

Change
from $20? $____.____

Basic Math Skills 3

BANANA SPLITS!

ice cream	**60¢** each scoop
banana	**20¢** per piece
chocolate sauce	**15¢**
whipping cream	**24¢**
walnuts	**18¢**
cherry	**10¢** each

1. 1 scoop ice cream
   chocolate sauce
   2 pieces banana
   1 cherry

cost $ ____ . ____

2. 1 scoop ice cream
   1 piece banana
   whipping cream
   walnuts

cost $ ____ . ____

3. 2 scoops ice cream
   2 banana pieces
   chocolate sauce
   whipping cream

cost $ ____ . ____

4. 3 scoops ice cream
   2 pieces banana
   whipping cream
   3 cherries

cost $ ____ . ____

5.   Make your own.

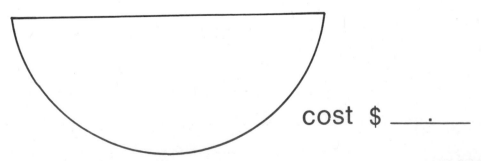

cost $ ____ . ____

Basic Math Skills 3

WHAT DOES YOUR NAME COST?

vowels $1.00 a e i o u	"tail" letters $ .75 g j p q y	all other letters $ .35

1. M a r y	2. L e o n	3. S u e
$ .35 1.00 .35 + .75 —— $.		

4. E m i l y	5. Your first name	6. Your last name

     Basic Math Skills 3

1. $29.98 $67.24 $38.47 $46.22
   + 12.79   + 12.79   + 49.22   + 34.87

2. $48.64 $57.20 $80.90 $30.00
   - 21.39   - 46.19   - 61.82   - 19.95

3. one dollar minus three quarters $ ___ . ___

4. three dollars plus five dimes $ ___ . ___

5. eight dollars times seven $ ___ . ___

6. five dollars plus four quarters $ ___ . ___

7. ten dollars minus ninety pennies $ ___ . ___

130   Basic Math Skills 3

HOW MUCH DID I EARN?

1. Earl
$ _____._____

2. Olive
$ _____._____

3. Marilyn
$ _____._____

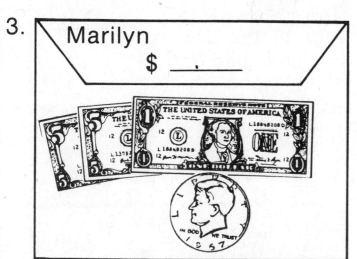

4. Clifford
$ _____._____

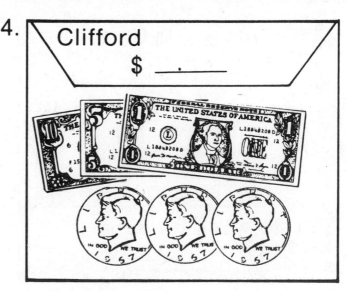

5. William
$ _____._____

6. Janice
$ _____._____

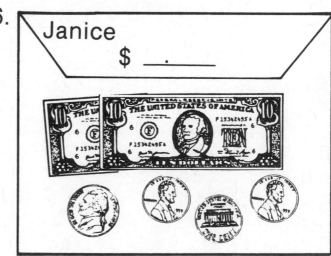

7. Who earned the most? _____

8. Who earned the least? _____

Basic Math Skills 3

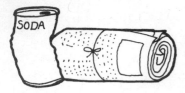 # RECYCLE FOR MONEY!

1. Missy collected 24 cans. She got 3¢ for each can. How much did she earn?

2. Joyce collected 20 pounds of glass. She got 5¢ for each pound. How much did she earn?

3. Philip earned 39¢ collecting aluminum cans. He got 3¢ for each can. How many cans did he collect?

4. Raymond collected 9 soda bottles. His friend B.J. collected 8. Each bottle was worth 10¢. How much did they earn together?

5. Thomas found 8 soda bottles for 10¢ each and 12 aluminum cans for 3¢ each. How much did he earn?

6. Rachel earned $2.55 collecting glass. She got 5¢ for each pound. How many pounds did she collect?

7. Bobbie earned $4.00 collecting soda bottles. She got 10¢ for each bottle. How many bottles did she collect?

8. Sammy collected 10 pounds of newspapers every day for 4 days. He got 12¢ a pound for the papers. How much did he earn in all?

Basic Math Skills 3

Sandwich **$1.25**   Milk **$ .50**
Hot dog **$1.00**   Apple juice **$ .70**
Fish and chips **$2.50**   Hot chocolate **$ .60**
Cookie **$ .15** OR **2 for $ .25**

1.

sandwich $ ___.___
milk $ ___.___
2 cookies $ ___.___

total cost $ ___.___

2.

2 hot dogs $ ___.___
apple juice $ ___.___
cookie $ ___.___

total cost $ ___.___

3.

2 sandwiches $ ___.___
1 hot chocolate $ ___.___
1 milk $ ___.___
4 cookies $ ___.___

total cost $ ___.___

4. I have $5.00. I bought fish and chips, apple juice, and 4 cookies. How much change will I get back?

$ ___.___

5. What would you buy for lunch? What would it cost?

total cost $ ___.___

6. What could you buy for exactly $2.00?

ARTURO'S BUDGET

1. Income

allowance	$ 5.00
sister paid back a loan	$ 2.75
earned mowing lawns	$10.00
earned baby-sitting	$ 3.75
collected aluminum cans	$ 1.63

2. Expenses

school supplies: $ ___.___

    notebook $1.15
    pencils   .65

bought birthday present: $ ___.___

    gift $4.58
    bow   .50
    paper   1.05
    card   .40

library fine $ 1.56

ice cream $ ___.___
    2 — $.90 each

deposit to savings account $ 10.00

lost money at park: $ ___.___
    3 nickels

---

3. How much was Arturo's total income? _____

4. How much were his total expenses? _____

5. How much cash does he have left? _____

ALONG THE MONEY TRAIL

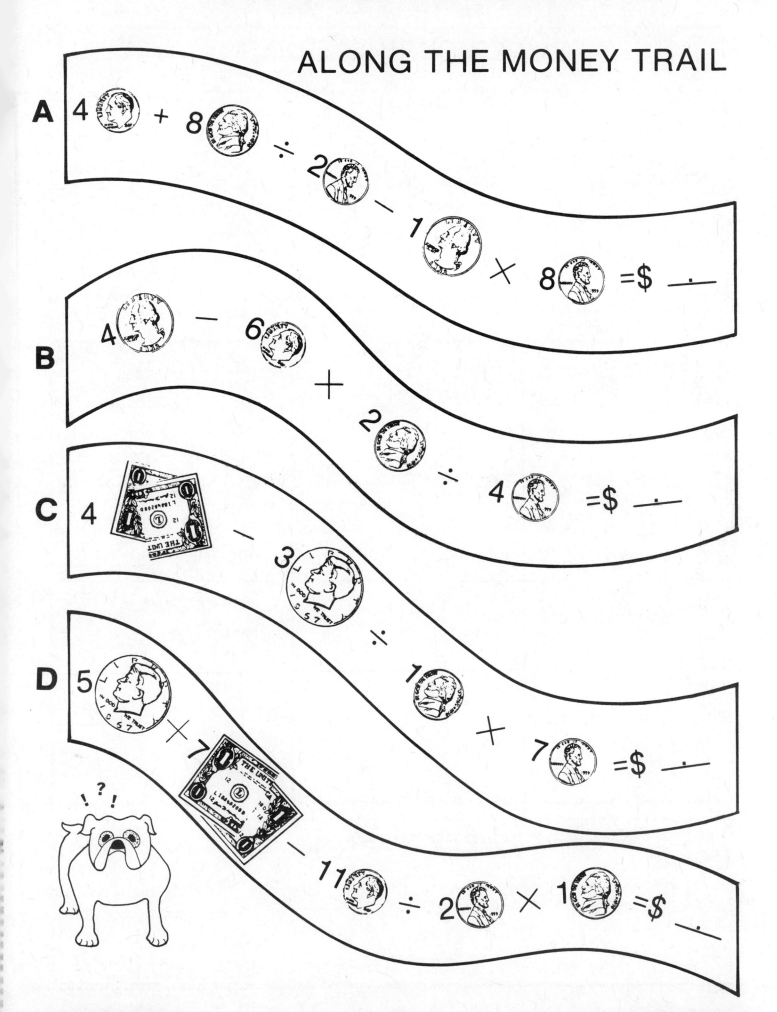

A 4 🪙 + 8 🪙 ÷ 2 🪙 − 1 🪙 × 8 🪙 = $ _____ . _____

B 4 🪙 − 6 🪙 + 2 🪙 ÷ 4 🪙 = $ _____ . _____

C 4 💵 − 3 🪙 ÷ 1 🪙 × 7 🪙 = $ _____ . _____

D 5 🪙 + 7 💵 − 11 🪙 ÷ 2 🪙 × 1 🪙 = $ _____ . _____

Basic Math Skills 3

SUPER SPRING SALE!

KITES 1/3 off

$12.00

$9.60

WHEELS 1/2 off

$68.00

$14.00

$22.40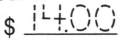

BOOKS 1/4 off

$4.00 $2.00

---

1. skateboard

cost $ 14.00

amount
off $ 7.00
sale

price $ 7.00

2. big book

cost $ ___.___

amount
off $ ___.___
sale

price $ ___.___

3. bat kite

cost $ ___.___

amount
off $ ___.___
sale

price $ ___.___

4. bike

cost $ ___.___

amount
off $ ___.___
sale

price $ ___.___

5. fish kite

cost $ ___.___

amount
off $ ___.___
sale

price $ ___.___

6. roller skates

cost $ ___.___

amount
off $ ___.___
sale

price $ ___.___

SUPER BONUS!!!

What would you pay if you bought one of each thing?

$___.___

Basic Math Skills 3

Word Problems

These pages have been developed to give students the opportunity to apply math skills to word problems. Each page may be completed by individual students or used by the teacher as a whole group activity.

Students should be encouraged to:

1. Read the problem.

2. Think about possible solutions.

3. Work the problem and show their work.

4. Check their answers.

Answer Key

Page 139:	1. 9:30	2. 20	3. 16	4. 30	5. 64	6. 45 min	**Bonus:** 34
Page 140:	1. 7	2. 33	3. 116	4. 6	5. 225	6. $2.26	**Bonus:** Answers will vary.
Page 141:	1. 3	2. 90	3. 67	4. 152	5. $6.91	6. $1.00	**Bonus:** $2.80
Page 142:	1. 15	2. 8	3. 30	4. 7	5. 18	6. 4	**Bonus:** 22
Page 143:	1. 14 ¢	2. 17 ¢	3. 9 ¢	4. 7 ¢	5. 5 ¢	6. yes	**Bonus:** 70 ¢, change 5 ¢
Page 144:	1. 4	2. 17	3. 9	4. 17	5. 16	6. 5	**Bonus:** 250 300
							350 400
Page 145:	1. 12	2. 26	3. $23	4. 5	5. $1	6. 14	**Bonus:** 21
Page 146:	1. 16	2. 18	3. 7	4. 14	5. 18	6. 18	**Bonus:** 3, 2, 4
Page 147:	1. 22	2. 4	3. 40	4. 75 ¢	5. 45	6. 5 ¢	**Bonus:** 15
Page 148:	1. 32	2. 88	3. 24	4. 22	5. 20	6. 36	**Bonus:** Answers will vary.
Page 149:	1. $19.75	2. $1.15	3. $2.96	4. 90 ¢	5. $3.95	6. Yes, he still has $10.14	**Bonus:** $48
Page 150:	1. Sun Bear Polar Bear Polar Bear	2. Black Bear Spectacled Bear	3. 260	4. 4 feet	5. 690	6. 30	**Bonus:** 200
Page 151:	1. 6	2. 3	3. 5	4. 4	5. 6	6. 8	**Bonus:** 2, 9, 2, 6
Page 152:	1. 37	2. 599	3. 23	4. 12	5. 8	6. $14	**Bonus:** 40
Page 153:	1. 14	2. 5	3. 1 foot	4. 69	5. 86	6. 2	**Bonus:** 46 69 120 180 40 60
Page 154:	1. 15	2. 9:30	3. 55	4. 2:45	5. 7:35	6. 7:00	**Bonus:** 1:00 5:00 3:30 7:30 7:17 11:17 11:25 3:25
Page 155:	1. $4.75	2. $3.05	3. $1.70	4. 10 ¢	5. 90 ¢	6. $15.95	**Bonus:** 20
Page 156:	1. 18	2. 60	3. 35	4. 35	5. 90	6. 6	**Bonus:** 84
Page 157:	1. Bronto-saurus 70 feet	2. Stego-saurus Triceratops	3. 15	4. 35	5. 205	6. 20	**Bonus:** Stegosaurus Tyrannosaurus Rex Triceratops
Page 158:	1. 3	2. 3, 000	3. 600	4. 8	5. 9	6. 9	**Bonus:** 3, 500
Page 159:	1. 522	2. 304	3. 24	4. 31 ¢	5. 12	6. 7	**Bonus:** 31 35 39 47
Page 160:	1. $27	2. $2.00	3. 4	4. 4 1/2	5. 2 4 6 8 10 4 8 12 16 20 6 12 18 24 30	6. 11 ¢	**Bonus:** $9
Page 161:	1. 137	2. 300	3. 49	4. 134 million	5. 322	6. 7, 600	**Bonus:** 7, 000, 000, 000
Page 162:	1. 115	2. 40	3. 9	4. 30	5. 10	6. 1	**Bonus:** 4'9"
Page 163:	1. $900	2. $18	3. 3	4. 81	5. 9	6. $860 $40	**Bonus:** 44
Page 164:	1. 54	2. 6	3. 63	4. 45	5. 8	6. $3	**Bonus:** 28
Page 165:	1. $6	2. $4.25	3. $1.75	4. 10 ¢	5. $1.95	6. 6:00	**Bonus:** 2 4 10 20 4 8 20 40
Page 166:	1. 42	2. 8	3. 72	4. 179	5. 72 ¢	6. 5	**Bonus:** 16
Page 167:	1. Sunday Tuesday Saturday Wednesday	2. 5 31 9 21	3. 23 8	4. 24 Thursday	5. 63	6. 730	**Bonus:** 36 1825
Page 168:	1. 55	2. 7:55	3. 8:50	4. 40	5. 10	6. 40 11	**Bonus:** 3:30 4:30 3:00 4:00 5:45 6:45 11:15 12:15
Page 169:	1. 227	2. 108	3. 38	4. 114	5. 8:50	6. 249	**Bonus:** 18 23 28 33
Page 170:	1. 3	2. Depends on the year	3. 190	4. 10:47	5. 732	6. 1347	**Bonus:** Wilber - 36 Orville - 32 4 years
Page 171:	1. 270 tons	2. 806	3. 100	4. 12,000	5. 350	6. 60	**Bonus:** 24,304
Page 172:	1. $18.03	2. $1.69	3. 9	4. 36	5. 2 hrs 15min	6. $15	**Bonus:** 1474 1574 1674 1774

Basic Math Skills 3

Visiting a Farm

1. Scout Troop 27 went on a trip to a farm. They left at 9:00. It took 30 minutes to get to the farm. What time did they get there?

   _____

2. The boys milked a cow. 5 quarts of milk go into the pail. If each quart is 4 cups, how many cups of milk are in the pail?

   _____

3. Mrs. Brown made cookies for the scouts. There were 63 cookies. The boys ate 47. How many cookies were left?

   _____

4. Farmer Brown has 6 rabbits. Each rabbit has 5 babies. How many baby rabbits are there?

   _____

5. They picked up eggs. The boys found 28 brown eggs and 36 white eggs. How many eggs did they have?

   _____

6. At 3:00 the scout troop started for home. When they got home, the clock looked like this. How long did it take to get home?

   _____

BONUS: Farmer Brown's prize pig had 6 babies. One weighed 8 pounds, four weighed 5 pounds each and one weighed 6 pounds. What was the total weight of the piglets?

At the Zoo

1. Elephant was 11 feet tall. Giraffe was 18 feet tall. How much taller was the giraffe?

   _____

4. Boa was 33 feet long. Python was 27 feet long. How much shorter is the python?

   _____

2. 72 monkeys are in the tree. 39 monkeys are under the tree. How many more are in the tree?

   _____

5. 590 people came to the zoo on Saturday. 365 people came today. How many more came on Saturday?

   _____

3. A baby elephant is 233 pounds. A baby giraffe is 117 pounds. How much less is the giraffe baby?

   _____

6. It costs $6.52 to feed the hippo and $4.26 to feed the bear. How much more does it cost to feed the hippo?

   _____

BONUS: Ask 10 people, "What animal do you like best at the zoo?" Make a list of the animals they pick. Make a ring around the animal most people pick.

Bubbles' New Home

1. Terry made a new home for her dog, Bubbles. She got 6-foot-long boards. She cut each board in half. How long was each part?

   _____

2. It took 10 minutes to cut each board. How long did it take to cut 9 boards? (Hint: Count by 10s.)

   _____

3. Terry got 164 nails. She used 97. How many nails were left?

   _____

4. It took 98 minutes to make the walls and 54 minutes to put on the roof. How long did Terry work?

   _____

5. She got two cans of paint. Green was $2.56. White was $4.35. How much did the paint cost?

   _____

6. She got a dish that said, "Bubbles." It cost $4.00. How much did she get back from $5.00?

   _____

BONUS: Bubbles ate dog food that cost $.40 a day. How much did it cost to feed Bubbles for one week?

         Basic Math Skills 3

Back to School

1. 9 boys in my class ride the bus to school. 6 girls ride the bus. How many in my class ride the bus to school? _____	2. There were 17 girls in Mrs. Baker's class last year. Now there are 9 girls. How many more girls did she have last year? _____
3. Room 9 has 5 rows of desks. Each row has 6 desks in it. How many desks in all? (Hint: Count by 5s.) _____	4. There are 14 children in my reading group. Half are boys. How many boys are there? _____
5. 5 boys sit in row one. 3 boys sit in row two. 6 boys sit in row three. 4 boys sit in row four. How many boys are in the class? _____	6. Mrs. Alanzo has taught 9 years. Mrs. Baker taught third grade for 7 years and fourth grade for 6 years. How much longer has Mrs. Baker taught? _____

BONUS: There were 358 students at Bayview School last year.
There are 336 students this year.
How many more students came to Bayview last year?

 Basic Math Skills 3

Snack Time

1. A muffin costs 7¢. How much will 2 muffins cost?

   _____

2. Sherry bought a muffin for 7¢ and milk for 10¢. How much did she spend in all?

   _____

3. Brian wants apple juice. It costs 18¢. He has 9¢. How much more does he need?

   _____

4. An orange costs 8¢. A pear costs 15¢. How much more is the pear?

   _____

5. Bert bought a cookie that cost 5¢. He gave the clerk a dime. How much money did he get back?

   _____

6. Clyde wants an apple that costs 15¢. He has a dime and a nickel. Can he buy the apple?

   _____

BONUS: One muffin costs 7¢. How much will 10 cost?

If you paid with three quarters, how much change would you get back?

       Basic Math Skills 3

Field Day

1. 13 boys and 9 girls were in the broad jump contest. How many more boys were in the contest?

　　　　　　　　　＿＿＿＿

2. Each person got 3 jumps. George jumped 4 feet on his first try. He jumped 8 feet on his second try and 5 feet on his last try. How far did he jump in all?

　　　　　　　　　＿＿＿＿

3. Arthur only made 9 baskets in the contest last year. This year he got the ball through the hoop 18 times. How many more baskets did he make this year?

　　　　　　　　　＿＿＿＿

4. Sherry threw the baseball 8 yards, then 9 yards. How far did she throw the ball in all?

　　　　　　　　　＿＿＿＿

5. 8 teams were in the 3-legged race. Each team had 2 children. How many children were in the race?
(Hint: Count by 2s.)

　　　　　　　　　＿＿＿＿

6. 16 children were in the beanbag toss. 4 hit the center of the target. 7 hit the edge of the target. How many missed the target?

　　　　　　　　　＿＿＿＿

BONUS:　100　150　200　＿＿＿　＿＿＿　＿＿＿　＿＿＿　450

Basic Math Skills 3

Bikes

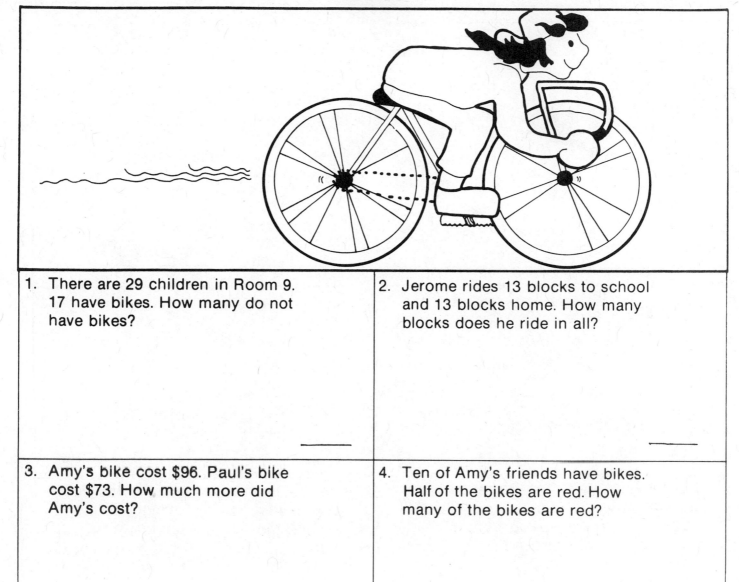

1. There are 29 children in Room 9. 17 have bikes. How many do not have bikes?

   _____

2. Jerome rides 13 blocks to school and 13 blocks home. How many blocks does he ride in all?

   _____

3. Amy's bike cost $96. Paul's bike cost $73. How much more did Amy's cost?

   _____

4. Ten of Amy's friends have bikes. Half of the bikes are red. How many of the bikes are red?

   _____

5. Jerome bought new tires for $21, a bell for $5, and a basket for $13. How much will he get back from $40?

   _____

6. Harry rides his bike 2 miles every day. How many miles does he ride in a week?

   _____

BONUS: Paul rides his bike 5 miles each day. Jerome rides his bike 2 miles each day. How many more miles will Paul ride in a week?

Basic Math Skills 3

Pirate's Treasure

1. Captain Crook and his crew sailed across the sea looking for a lost treasure chest. It was sunny 9 days of the trip and stormy 7 days. How long did they sail?

   _____

2. The pirates landed a small boat on shore. Then they walked 6 miles to a cave, 5 miles around the cave and 7 miles to some palm trees. How far did they go?

   _____

3. 4 pirates hid behind the palm trees and 2 stayed in the cave. If there were 13 pirates in all, how many went on to the grass hut?

   _____

4. From the grass hut, Captain Crook and his men went south 8 miles, then west 6 miles to a small lagoon. How far was the lagoon from the grass hut?

   _____

5. It took 10 minutes to row the canoe to the hill in the middle of the lagoon. Then 8 more minutes to find the treasure chest. How many minutes did it take in all?

   _____

6. When the pirates opened the treasure chest, they found 6 bars of gold, 4 long silver chains and 8 diamond necklaces. How many pieces of treasure did they find?

   _____

BONUS: Captain Crook kept half of the treasure for himself. How much did he keep?

_____ bars of gold

_____ silver chains

_____ diamond necklaces

Halloween Carnival

1. Our class made 98 paper chains to decorate for the Halloween carnival. We used 76. How many were left?

   _____

2. The carnival began at 5:30. It ended at 9:30. How many hours did the carnival last?

   _____

3. Carnival tickets were 10 for $1. How many can I get for $4?

   _____

4. Jenny got hungry while playing games. She got a hot dog for 50¢ and punch for 25¢. How much did she spend?

   _____

5. There were 59 balloons. Tracy threw darts at the balloons and broke 14. How many balloons were left?

   _____

6. Popcorn cost 35¢. Pete gave the clerk 4 dimes. How much money did he get back?

   _____

BONUS: Carmen liked the ring-toss game. She paid 5 tickets for 3 rings. How many tickets did she use for 9 rings?

Basic Math Skills 3

C is for Cats

Jaguar   **Snow Leopard**   **Cheetah**   **Ocelot**

1. An ocelot's body is 40 inches long. A jaguar's body is 72 inches long. How much longer is the jaguar?

   _____

2. A small bobcat weighs 11 pounds. A small cheetah weighs 77 pounds. How much do they weigh together?

   _____

3. The snow leopard has a 35-inch tail. A jungle cat has an 11-inch tail. How much longer is the tail of the snow leopard?

   _____

4. Tammi has 3 house cats. The Siamese weighs 9 pounds. The Tabby weighs 7 pounds. The Persian weighs 6 pounds. How much do they weigh together?

   _____

5. A cheetah can run 60 miles per hour for a short way. A greyhound dog can run 40 miles per hour. How much faster can the cheetah run?

   _____

6. Most cats have tails that are about 1 foot long. How many inches long would 3 cat tails be? (Remember how many inches are in 1 foot.)

   _____

BONUS: Ask 10 of your friends "Do you have a cat?" Then fill in this graph.

	yes	no
6		
5		
4		
3		
2		
1		

       Basic Math Skills 3

At the Toy Store

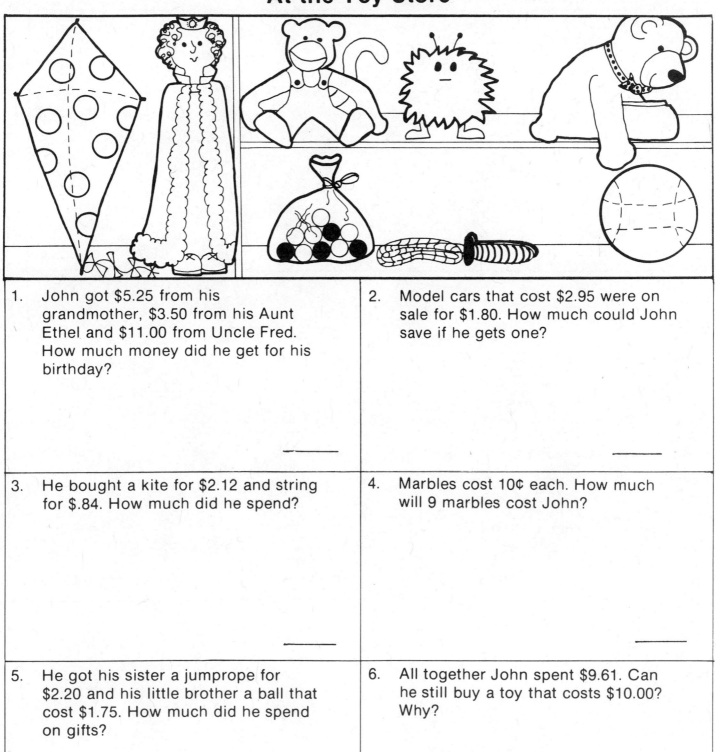

1. John got $5.25 from his grandmother, $3.50 from his Aunt Ethel and $11.00 from Uncle Fred. How much money did he get for his birthday?

2. Model cars that cost $2.95 were on sale for $1.80. How much could John save if he gets one?

3. He bought a kite for $2.12 and string for $.84. How much did he spend?

4. Marbles cost 10¢ each. How much will 9 marbles cost John?

5. He got his sister a jumprope for $2.20 and his little brother a ball that cost $1.75. How much did he spend on gifts?

6. All together John spent $9.61. Can he still buy a toy that costs $10.00? Why?

BONUS:

Martha got $24 for her birthday. Sally got twice as much as Martha. How much did Sally get?

Basic Math Skills 3

Bears! Bears! Bears!

	Black Bear	Grizzly Bear	Polar Bear	Sun Bear	Spectacled Bear
Height in feet	5	9	10	4	5
Weight in pounds	360	1,500	1,700	100	230

1. Which bear is shortest? _____

   Which bear is tallest? _____

   Which bear weighs the most?_____

2. Which two bears are about the same height?

   _____ and

   _____

3. How much heavier is the Black bear than the Sun bear?

   _____

4. The Grizzly bear is how much taller than the Black bear?

   _____

5. What is the weight of a Black bear, Sun bear and a Spectacled bear all together?

   _____

6. How much more does a Black bear weigh than the Sun bear and Spectacled bear together?

   _____

BONUS: What is the difference in weight between the Polar bear and the Grizzly bear?

                   Basic Math Skills 3

Concepts: fractional parts (1/2, 1/3, 1/4); dozen

Fun With Fractions

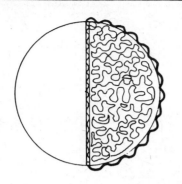 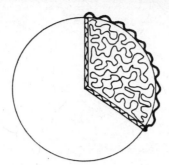 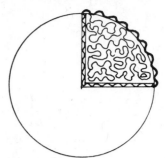

1/2   **1/3**   **1/4**

1. Joy had 12 pennies. She gave half to Tom. How many did she keep?

   ___

2. Mary had 9 stickers. 1/3 were animal stickers. How many animal stickers did she have?

   ___

3. There were 15 shells on the beach. Paul, Jose and Bill each took the same number. How many shells did each boy take?

   ___

4. Katy had a carrot to feed the ponies at the farm. She fed 1/4 of the carrot to each pony. How many ponies can she give a piece of carrot to?

   ___

5. How many apples do you get in 1/2 dozen?

   ___

6. Mom baked a cake for Albert's birthday. Three friends came to his party. Each boy ate two pieces. How many pieces did Mom need to cut the cake into?
   (Don't forget to count Albert.)

   ___

BONUS:
Circle the correct number of shapes.

1/3   **3/4**   **2/5**   **6/8**

                   Basic Math Skills 3

Greatest Show on Earth

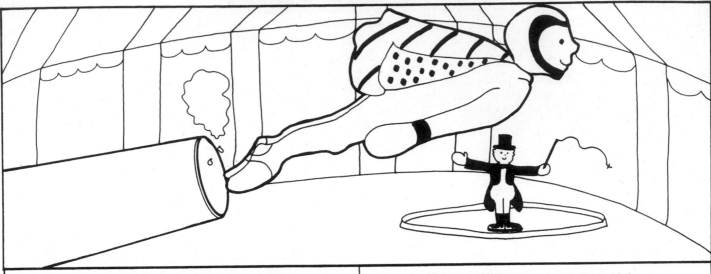

1. Wagner's Circus traveled by train. The circus needed 10 cars for animals, 11 cars for people and 16 cars for equipment. How many cars were in the train?

   _____

2. On Friday 235 boys and 364 girls from our school went to the circus. How many children is this?

   _____

3. The children saw a minibus full of clowns. 12 clowns got out of the bus. 11 clowns stayed on the bus. How many clowns were there in all?

   _____

4. Renaldo was shot out of a cannon. He flew 48 feet the first shot and 36 feet the second shot. How many more feet did he go the first shot?

   _____

5. The trapeze flyers practice 3 hours before lunch and 5 hours after lunch. How many hours a day do they practice?

   _____

6. Tickets cost $2 for children and $4 for adults. How much will it cost a family with two adults and three children?

   _____

BONUS: The trapeze flyers practice 5 days a week. How many hours a week do they practice? (Remember the answer to #5.)

Animal World Records

1. An anaconda snake is 25 feet long. A giant earthworm is 11 feet long. How much longer is the snake?

   _____

2. Whale shark eggs are 12 inches long. Ostrich eggs are 7 inches long. How much longer is the whale shark egg?

   _____

3. A bird-wing butterfly is 12 inches across. How many feet is this?

   _____

4. The slow little snail slides along at 23 inches an hour. How far can it go in three hours?

   _____

5. A spine-tailed swift flew 106 miles per hour. A racerunner lizard ran 20 miles per hour. How much faster did the swift move?

   _____

6. If a sailfish swam 22 miles in one hour, how many hours will it take the sailfish to swim 44 miles?

   _____

BONUS: How far can I go?

	1 hour	2 hours	3 hours
snail	23 inches		
cheetah	60 miles		
racing lizard	20 miles		

Basic Math Skills 3

Visiting Grandma

1. Marvin left home at 8:00. He got to the bus stop at 8:15. How many minutes did it take him to get there?

    _____

2. Marvin got on the bus at 8:30. It took 1 hour to get to Grandma's house. What time did he get there?

    _____

3. They went to the store. It took 20 minutes to get to the store, 15 minutes to shop and 20 minutes to get home. How long were they gone?

    _____

4. Grandma made a cake for dinner. It had to bake for 45 minutes. She put it in the oven at 2:00. What time did she take it out?

    _____

5. After dinner, Marvin helped by washing the dishes. He started at 7:15. It took him 20 minutes. What time did he finish?

    _____

6. Father came to get Marvin after dinner. It was a 2-hour drive. If he got there at 9:00, what time did he start?

    _____

BONUS: Fill in the boxes:

2 hours ago		2 hours later
	3:00	
	5:30	
	9:17	
	1:25	

Basic Math Skills 3

On the Way to the Bank

1. Angelica wanted to put some money into her savings account at the bank. She had $2.00 allowance, $1.25 from her piggy bank and $1.50 she made washing the car. How much money did she have?	2. She dropped her purse and spilled the money under a tree in the park. She found 1 dollar, 3 quarters, 8 dimes, 6 nickels and 20 pennies. How much did she find?
3. How much was still lost? (Remember the answers to #1 and #2.)	4. Ernest came along and helped look for the money. He found 2 quarters, 6 dimes, 8 nickels and 10 pennies. How much is still lost? (Remember the answer to #3.)
5. They went to the ice-cream shop. Angelica bought Ernest an ice-cream cone for helping her. His cost 55¢. Angelica's cost 35¢. How much did she spend?	6. She put $3.75 in her savings account. She already had $12.15 in the account. How much does she have now?

BONUS: How many quarters are there in 5 dollars?

155   Basic Math Skills 3

The Great Houdini

1. Harry Houdini was a great escape artist. In Russia he got out of iron bands and a locked police van in 28 minutes. In San Francisco he got out of 10 pairs of handcuffs in 10 minutes. How much faster was that escape?

   _____

2. In the Chinese Water Torture Cell trick, he escaped from the locked cabinet in 120 seconds. He escaped from the Water Can trick in 180 seconds. How much longer did it take him to get out of the water can?

   _____

3. Houdini only slept 5 hours a night. How many hours did he sleep in a week? (Don't forget how many days are in a week.)

   _____

4. Houdini was only 17 years old when he became a magician. He performed until he was 52. How many years was he a magician?

   _____

5. If it took Houdini 9 seconds to escape from one pair of handcuffs, how long will it take him to get out of 10 pairs?

   _____

6. He often went many hours without eating. He then would gobble down 2 quarts of milk mixed with a dozen eggs. How many eggs were in each quart of milk?
   (Remember - 12 is one dozen.)

   _____

BONUS: It took a lot of practice for Houdini to learn a new escape. If he practiced 6 hours a day for 14 days, how many hours would he have practiced?

Basic Math Skills 3

Dinosaurs

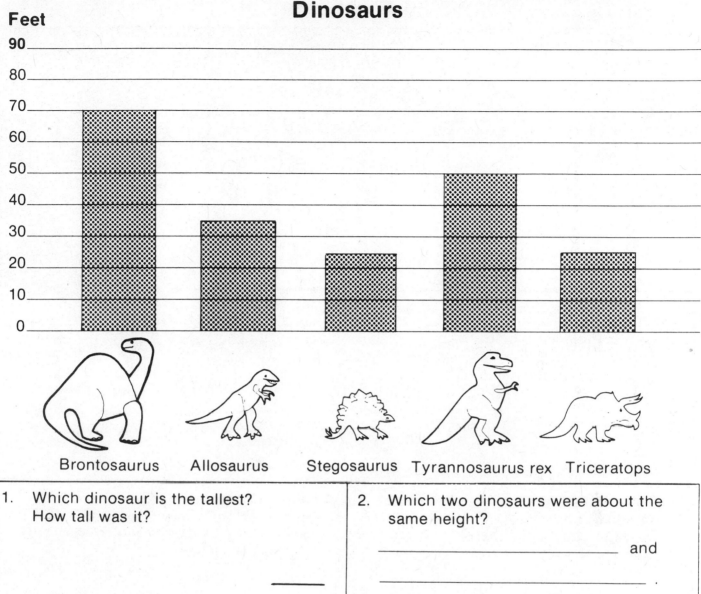

1.	Which dinosaur is the tallest? How tall was it? _____	2.	Which two dinosaurs were about the same height? _____ and _____ .
3.	How much taller was Tyrannosaurus rex than Allosaurus? _____	4.	How much shorter was Allosaurus than Brontosaurus? _____
5.	How tall would all five dinosaurs be if you put them together? _____	6.	Together Stegosaurus and Triceratops were how much shorter than Brontosaurus? _____

BONUS: Which 3 dinosaurs would equal 100 feet if put together?

Basic Math Skills 3

Elephants

African

Asian

1. Asian elephants can be as tall as 9 feet. African elephants can be as tall as 12 feet. How much taller is the African elephant?

   _____

2. An Asian elephant can weigh 6,000 pounds. An African elephant can weigh 9,000 pounds. How much less does the Asian elephant weigh?

   _____

3. If an elephant in a zoo eats 200 pounds of hay and other food in a day, how much will it eat in 3 days?

   _____

4. An elephant brain is about 11 pounds. Your brain is about 3 pounds. How much larger is the elephant's brain?

   _____

5. A baby elephant calf is about 3 feet tall when it is born. How much will it have to grow to be 12 feet tall as an adult?

   _____

6. There were three elephants in the zoo. Together they were 28 feet tall. The first elephant was 12 feet tall. The second elephant was 7 feet tall. How tall was the third elephant?

   _____

BONUS: If a wild elephant ate 500 pounds of bark, grass and leaves in one day, how much will it eat in a week?

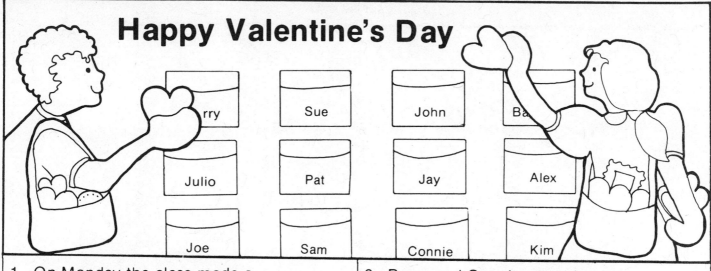

Happy Valentine's Day

1. On Monday the class made a large box for **valentines.** By Tuesday there were 124 in the box. Yesterday 148 were put in. Today 250 were put in. How many valentines are in the box now?

2. Barry and Connie passed out the valentine cards. If Barry passed out 218, how many will Connie have to pass out?
(Remember the answer to #1.)

3. Eight girls were making valentines. Each girl made 3. How many valentines did the girls make in all?

4. Danny bought valentines for all his friends. The valentines cost $1.69. How much change did Danny get back from $2.00?

5. 4 children brought the teacher flowers. Each child gave her 3 flowers. How many flowers did the teacher get?

6. Ginger baked 3 dozen cookies. There are 29 children in the class. If each child ate one cookie, how many cookies were left?

BONUS: What comes next?

19   23   27   ___   ___   43   ___

Basic Math Skills 3

Our New Pets

1. Charlie, Sam and George went to the SPCA to get kittens. It cost each boy $9 to get a kitten. What was the total cost of the kittens?

   _____

2. Charlie found a sale on cans of cat food. Each can cost $.40. How much did he pay for 5 cans?

   _____

3. Charlie's kitten gained 1 pound a week for 4 weeks. How many pounds did the kitten gain in all?

   _____

4. George's kitten weighed 2½ pounds when he got the kitten. In three weeks the kitten gained 2 pounds. How much did the kitten weigh then?

   _____

5. Fill in the blanks:

kittens	1	2	3	4	5
ears	2			8	
legs	4		12		
whiskers	6				30

6. Sam bought a toy mouse for $.75 and catnip for $.39. He gave the clerk $1.25. How much change did he get back?

   _____

BONUS: George bought a collar, a bed and a bag of kitty litter for his new pet. He gave the clerk $10. If he got back $1 in change, how much was his bill?

Basic Math Skills 3

The Solar System

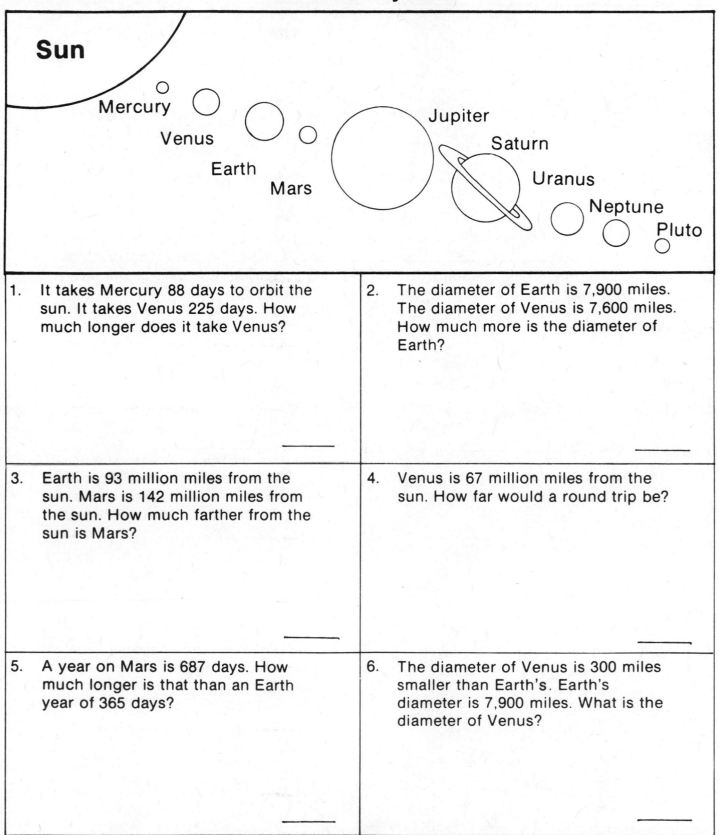

Sun

Mercury

Venus

Earth

Mars

Jupiter

Saturn

Uranus

Neptune

Pluto

1. It takes Mercury 88 days to orbit the sun. It takes Venus 225 days. How much longer does it take Venus?

_____

2. The diameter of Earth is 7,900 miles. The diameter of Venus is 7,600 miles. How much more is the diameter of Earth?

_____

3. Earth is 93 million miles from the sun. Mars is 142 million miles from the sun. How much farther from the sun is Mars?

_____

4. Venus is 67 million miles from the sun. How far would a round trip be?

_____

5. A year on Mars is 687 days. How much longer is that than an Earth year of 365 days?

_____

6. The diameter of Venus is 300 miles smaller than Earth's. Earth's diameter is 7,900 miles. What is the diameter of Venus?

_____

BONUS: Pluto is 3,500,000,000 miles from the sun. How many miles would a space ship have to travel to go from Pluto to the sun and back again?

161 Basic Math Skills 3

Mighty Mike

1. Mike could only lift 35 pounds when he started weight lifting. Now he can lift 150 pounds. How much more can he lift now?

_____

2. He does 1 sit-up every 5 seconds. How long will it take him to do 8 sit-ups?

_____

3. Yesterday Mike did 54 chin-ups in 6 minutes. How many chin-ups did he do in one minute?

_____

4. Mike used to ride his exercise bike 15 minutes each morning. Now he rides it twice as long. How many minutes does he ride now?

_____

5. How many times will Mike have to lift a 9-pound weight in his left hand to equal 90 pounds?

_____

6. Jumping rope is his favorite exercise. He jumps 20 minutes three times a week. How many hours a week does he jump rope?

_____

BONUS: Mike has grown 3 inches this year. He is now 5 feet tall. How tall was he last year?

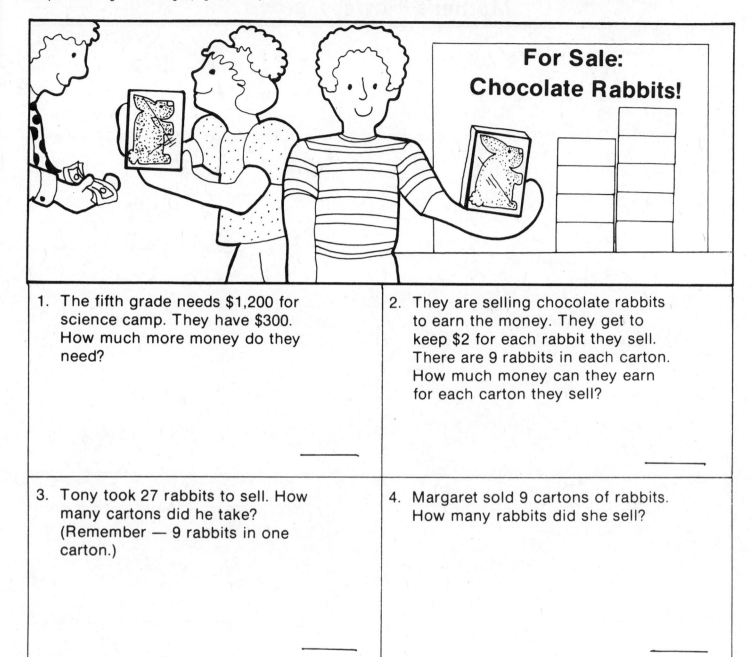

For Sale: Chocolate Rabbits!

1. The fifth grade needs $1,200 for science camp. They have $300. How much more money do they need?

   _____

2. They are selling chocolate rabbits to earn the money. They get to keep $2 for each rabbit they sell. There are 9 rabbits in each carton. How much money can they earn for each carton they sell?

   _____

3. Tony took 27 rabbits to sell. How many cartons did he take? (Remember — 9 rabbits in one carton.)

   _____

4. Margaret sold 9 cartons of rabbits. How many rabbits did she sell?

   _____

5. Two cartons were knocked over. Half of the chocolate rabbits were broken. How many rabbits were **not** broken?

   _____

6. The children sold 430 chocolate rabbits. How much money did they make? How much more money do they need for science camp? (Remember the answer to question #1.)

   _____

BONUS:

Kristie sold one dozen more rabbits than Carlos and Brian sold together.

Carlos sold 20 and Brian sold 12. How many did Kristie sell?

 Basic Math Skills 3

Mother's Flower Garden

1. Mother bought 9 boxes of flowers. Each box had 6 plants in it. How many flowers did she get?

   _____

2. There were 54 marigolds in 9 boxes. How many marigolds were in each box?

   _____

3. Mother got 54 pink petunias and 9 purple petunias. How many petunias did she buy?

   _____

4. 9 flowers were large. 54 flowers were small. How many more small flowers were there?

   _____

5. Mother had 48 geraniums. She planted 6 in a row. How many rows did she plant?

   _____

6. Some flowers were on sale at 5 for $.75. What will 20 flowers cost?

   _____

BONUS: Mother planted 8 rows of flowers this year. Each row

had 9 flowers in it. Last year she planted 100 flowers.

How many more did she plant last year?

     Basic Math Skills 3

Saturday at the Ball Game

1. It will cost $2.00 for each ticket to the game. How much will 3 tickets cost?

   _____

2. Ted has 2 dollars, 5 quarters, 7 dimes and 6 nickels. How much money does he have?

   _____

3. How much more money does Ted need to buy a ticket for himself, his sister and his brother? (Remember the answers to #1 and #2.)

   _____

4. Ted wants popcorn that costs $.65 and soda that costs $.50. How much change will he get if he gives the clerk $1.25?

   _____

5. How much would popcorn cost for all 3 children? (Remember popcorn costs $.65 a box.)

   _____

6. Father picked the children up after the game. If the game began at 3:30 and lasted 2½ hours, what time should Father get to the stadium?

   _____

BONUS: Fill in the boxes:

	half dollar	quarter	dime	nickel
$ .50	1	2	5	10
$1.00				
$2.00				

Basic Math Skills 3

At the Candy Store

Ye Olde Sweet Shop

1. There are 6 lollipops in a box. There are 7 boxes. How many lollipops are there?

_____

2. There are 48 gumdrops in all. There are 6 gumdrops in each bag. How many bags are there?

_____

3. Sylvia bought 8 packages of gum. There were 9 sticks of gum in each package. How many sticks of gum did she get?

_____

4. A jar of jellybeans is on the shelf. There are 63 red jellybeans, 89 green ones and 27 yellow ones. How many jellybeans are in the jar?

_____

5. If one candy cane costs 8¢, how much will 9 cost?

_____

6. How many jaw breakers can I buy if each one costs 7¢, and I have a quarter, a nickel and 5 pennies?

_____

BONUS: Mr. Jones bought 100 licorice whips. He sold one dozen each day last week. How many licorice whips did he have left?

       Basic Math Skills 3

Use this **calendar** to answer these questions.

	Sun.	Mon.	Tues.	Wed.	Thurs.	Fri.	Sat.
National Gorilla Day			1	2	3	4	5
	6	7	8	9	10	11	12
	13	14	15	16	17	18	19
	20	21	22	23	24	25	26
	27	28	29	30	31		

1. What day of the week is:

    13 _____

    22 _____

    19 _____

    30 _____

    _____

2. What is the date of:

    first Saturday _____

    last Thursday _____

    second Wednesday _____

    third Monday _____

    _____

3. How many days in this month are school days? _____
How many days are weekend days? _____

    _____

4. Amy's birthday is on the 10th. Paul's birthday is two weeks later. What is the **date** of Paul's birthday? _____
What **day of the week** is Paul's birthday? _____

    _____

5. If there are 7 days in each week, how many days are there in 9 weeks?

    _____

6. If there are 365 days in one year, how many days will there be in two years?

    _____

BONUS:

How many months are there in 3 years?

How many days are there in 5 years?

Basic Math Skills 3

Off to Work

1. In the morning it takes Dad 30 minutes to dress, 15 minutes to eat breakfast and 10 minutes to fix his lunch. How much time does he need?

   _____

2. If Dad gets up at 7:00, what time will he be ready for work?

   _____

3. Dad's store opens at 8:55. If he leaves home at 8:15 and it takes 35 minutes to get to the store, what time will he arrive at work?

   _____

4. He goes to lunch at 12:10. He has to be back by 12:50. How many minutes does he have to eat lunch?

   _____

5. Dad had one hour for a meeting. It took him 10 minutes to introduce everyone, 25 minutes to give his report and 15 minutes to answer questions. How many minutes were left? (Remember -an hour is 60 minutes.)

   _____

6. Dad works 8 hours a day for 5 days a week. How many hours a week does he work?_____
   If he worked 55 hours one week, how many hours a day would he have worked if he worked the same numbers of hours each day?

   _____

BONUS: Fill in the blanks.

½ hour ago		½ hour later
_____	4:00	_____
_____	3:30	_____
_____	6:15	_____
_____	11:45	_____

Basic Math Skills 3

Little League

1. There are 149 boys and 78 girls in the baseball league this year. What is the total number of players?
   _____

2. The Cardinals had batting practice today. Each player had a chance to swing at 12 balls. If 9 players came to practice, how many balls were pitched?
   _____

3. The Cardinals' coach drove the team to the game. It was 19 miles there and 19 miles back. How many miles did he drive?
   _____

4. How many miles would the coach drive if he had to make three trips? (Remember the answer to #3.)
   _____

5. The game between the Cardinals and the Pirates began at 6:30. The game lasted 2 hours and 20 minutes. What time was the game over?
   _____

6. The Cardinals had 27 hits in their first game, 23 hits in their second game and 19 hits in their last game. Last year they had a total of 318 hits. How many more hits will they need to make this year to have the same total as last year?
   _____

BONUS: Finish the pattern:

3   8   13   ____   ____   ____   38

The Flyer

1. Wilber and Orville Wright started trying to build a "flying machine" in 1900. They were successful in 1903. How many years did it take them?

2. The first flight took place in 1903. How many years ago was that?

3. The Wright brothers used the sand dunes near Kitty Hawk, North Carolina for glider experiments. Big Hill was 100 feet tall, Little Hill was 30 feet and West Hill was 60 feet. How high were the three sand dunes in all?

4. On Dec. 17, 1903 the Flyer lifted into the air at 10:35. This first flight lasted 12 seconds. What time did the plane land?

5. The Wright brothers made four flights that day. The shortest flight was 120 feet long. The longest flight was 852 feet long. What was the difference between the two flights?

6. What is the total number of feet the Flyer flew on Dec. 17 if the first flight was 120 feet, the second flight was 175 feet, the third flight was 200 feet and the last flight was 852 feet?

BONUS: Wilber was born in 1867. Orville was born in 1871. How old was each brother in 1903? How much older was Wilber than Orville?

Gray Whales

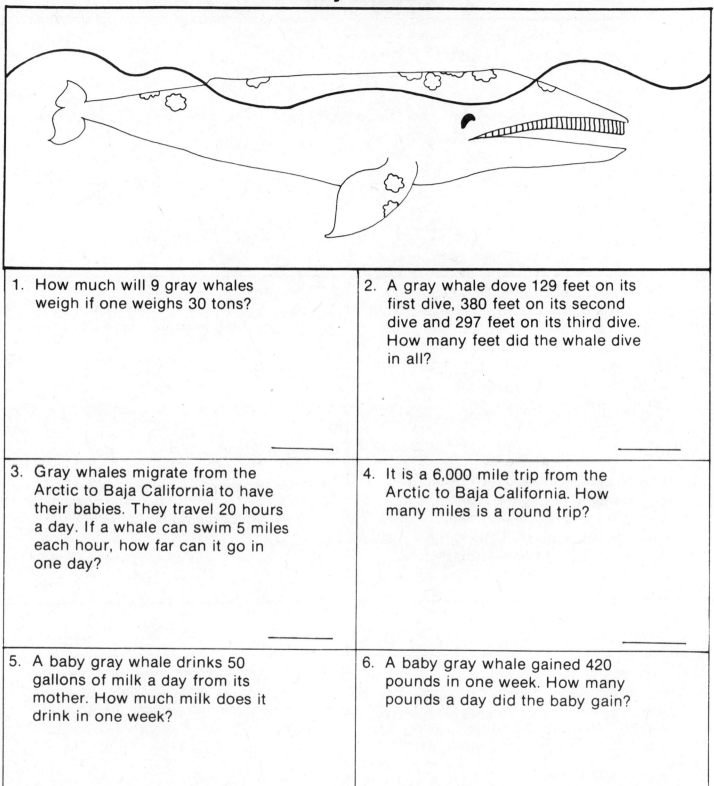

1. How much will 9 gray whales weigh if one weighs 30 tons?

_____

2. A gray whale dove 129 feet on its first dive, 380 feet on its second dive and 297 feet on its third dive. How many feet did the whale dive in all?

_____

3. Gray whales migrate from the Arctic to Baja California to have their babies. They travel 20 hours a day. If a whale can swim 5 miles each hour, how far can it go in one day?

_____

4. It is a 6,000 mile trip from the Arctic to Baja California. How many miles is a round trip?

_____

5. A baby gray whale drinks 50 gallons of milk a day from its mother. How much milk does it drink in one week?

_____

6. A baby gray whale gained 420 pounds in one week. How many pounds a day did the baby gain?

_____

BONUS: A **knot** is a measure of distance at sea. It is 6076 feet per hour.

A gray whale may cruise at 4 knots per hour. How many feet is this?

           Basic Math Skills 3

Huckleberry Finn's Raft Race

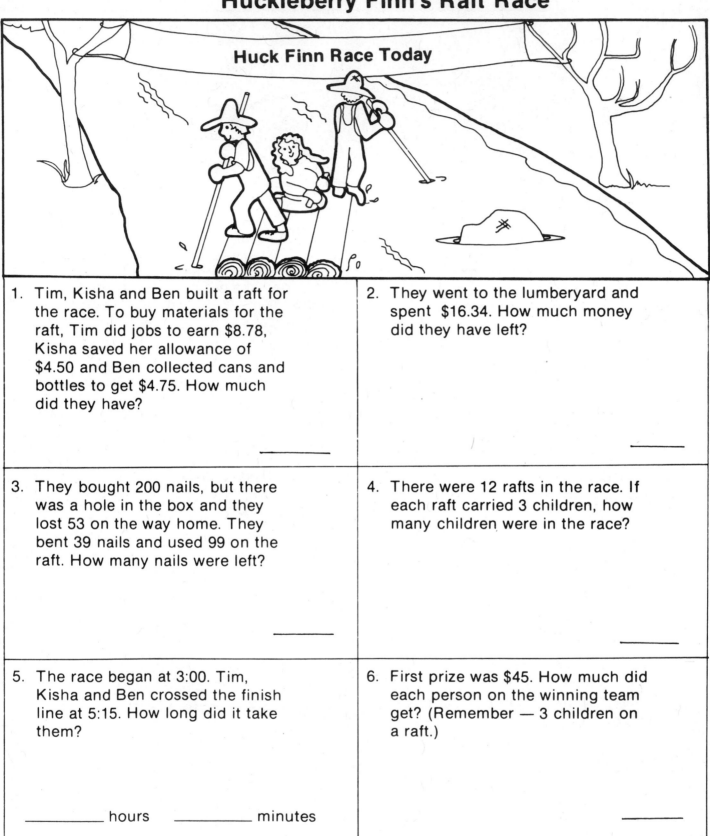

Huck Finn Race Today

1. Tim, Kisha and Ben built a raft for the race. To buy materials for the raft, Tim did jobs to earn $8.78, Kisha saved her allowance of $4.50 and Ben collected cans and bottles to get $4.75. How much did they have?

   _____

2. They went to the lumberyard and spent $16.34. How much money did they have left?

   _____

3. They bought 200 nails, but there was a hole in the box and they lost 53 on the way home. They bent 39 nails and used 99 on the raft. How many nails were left?

   _____

4. There were 12 rafts in the race. If each raft carried 3 children, how many children were in the race?

   _____

5. The race began at 3:00. Tim, Kisha and Ben crossed the finish line at 5:15. How long did it take them?

   _____ hours _____ minutes

6. First prize was $45. How much did each person on the winning team get? (Remember — 3 children on a raft.)

   _____

BONUS: What comes next?

1274   1374   _____   _____   _____   _____

Challenging
Math

This section contains a variety of interesting activities to challenge your students in many areas of math.

- *line segments*

- *counting challenges*

- *computation paths*

- *number puzzles*

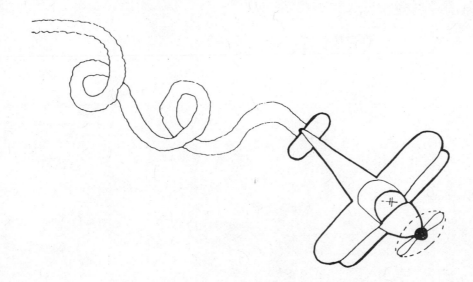

Basic Math Skills 3

Answer Key

Page 176

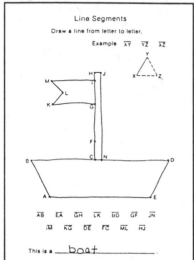

Page 177

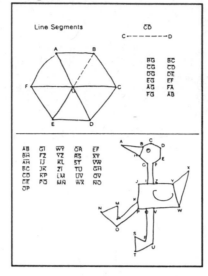

Page 178 (Answers will vary.)

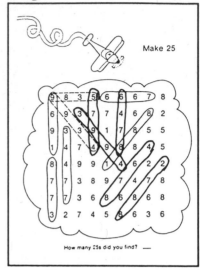

Page 179

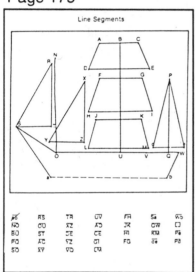

Page 180

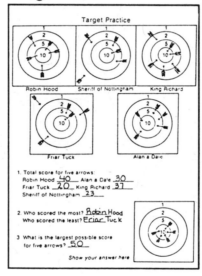

Page 181

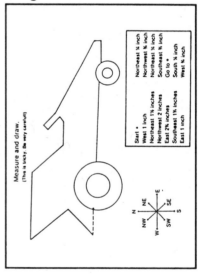

Page 182 - Dragon

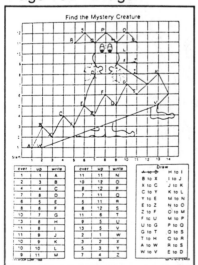

Page 183 - Pirate

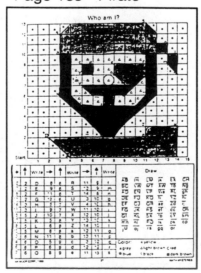

Page 184

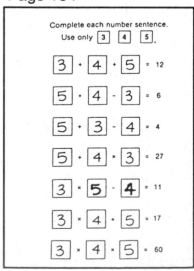

Basic Math Skills 3

(Answer key continued)

Page 185

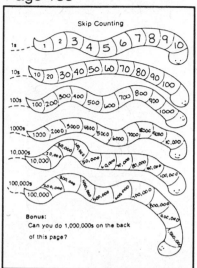

Skip Counting

1s: 1 2 3 4 5 6 7 8 9 10
10s: 10 20 30 40 50 60 70 80 90 100
100s: 100 200 300 400 500 600 700 800 900 1000
1000s: 1000 2000 3000 4000 5000 6000 7000 8000 9000 10,000
10,000s: 10,000 20,000 30,000 40,000 50,000 60,000 70,000 80,000 90,000 100,000
100,000s: 100,000 200,000 300,000 400,000 500,000 600,000 700,000 800,000 900,000 1,000,000

Bonus:
Can you do 1,000,000s on the back of this page?

Page 186

Math Paths

a. 1 + 2 + 3 + 4 + 5 = 15
b. 18 - 9 - 3 - 1 - 0 = 5
c. 1 × 1 × 2 × 2 × 5 = 20
d. 13 + 2 - 9 × 2 + 4 - 3 = 13
e. 3 × 3 - 3 + 3 × 3 = 27
f. 16 - 8 + 0 - 6 × 2 = 4

Page 187

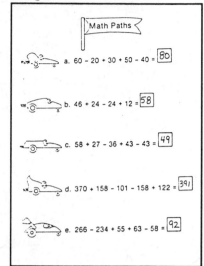

Math Paths

a. 60 - 20 + 30 + 50 - 40 = 80
b. 46 + 24 - 24 + 12 = 58
c. 58 + 27 - 36 + 43 - 43 = 49
d. 370 + 158 - 101 - 158 + 122 = 391
e. 266 - 234 + 55 + 63 - 58 = 92

Page 188

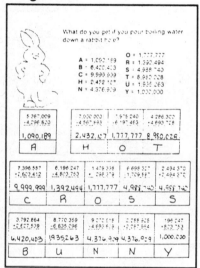

What do you get if you pour boiling water down a rabbit hole?

A = 1,090,189
B = 6,420,403
C = 9,999,999
H = 2,432,127
N = 4,376,909
O = 1,777,777
R = 1,392,494
S = 4,938,740
T = 8,960,028
U = 1,935,263
Y = 1,000,000

5,387,009 +4,396,620	7,000,000 +4,567,693	1,975,240 +6,197,463	4,286,300 +4,693,728
1,090,189	**2,432,127**	**1,777,777**	**8,960,028**
A	H	O	T

7,396,587 +2,603,412	6,196,247 +4,803,753	1,479,398 +2,298,379	6,698,327 +1,709,587	2,494,370 +2,494,370
9,999,999	**1,392,494**	**1,777,777**	**4,938,740**	**4,988,740**
C	R	O	S	S

3,792,864 +2,627,539	8,770,359 +6,635,096	9,070,618 +4,693,619	1,288,925 +2,297,864	196,247 +803,753
6,420,403	**1,935,263**	**4,376,909**	**4,376,909**	**1,000,000**
B	U	N	N	Y

Page 189

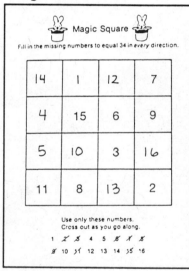

Magic Square

Fill in the missing numbers to equal 34 in *every* direction.

14	1	12	7
4	15	6	9
5	10	3	16
11	8	13	2

Use only these numbers.
Cross out as you go along.

~~1~~ ~~2~~ ~~3~~ 4 5 ~~6~~ ~~7~~ ~~8~~
~~9~~ 10 ~~11~~ 12 13 14 ~~15~~ 16

Page 190

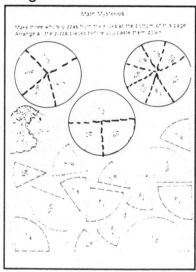

Math Mysteries

Make three whole pizzas from the slices at the bottom of the page. Arrange all the pizza pieces before you paste them down.

Page 191 (Answers will vary.)

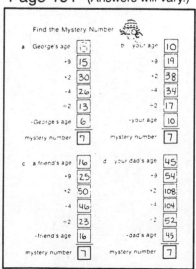

Find the Mystery Number

a. George's age: 6
+9: 15
×2: 30
-4: 26
÷2: 13
- George's age: 6
mystery number: 7

b. your age: 10
+9: 19
×2: 38
-4: 34
÷2: 17
- your age: 10
mystery number: 7

c. a friend's age: 16
+9: 25
×2: 50
-4: 46
÷2: 23
- friend's age: 16
mystery number: 7

d. your dad's age: 45
+9: 54
×2: 108
-4: 104
÷2: 52
- dad's age: 45
mystery number: 7

Page 192

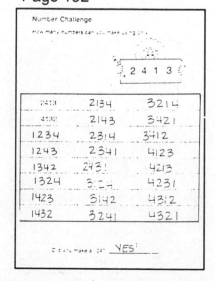

Number Challenge

How many numbers can you make using these?

2 4 1 3

2413	2134	3214
4132	2143	3421
1234	2314	3412
1243	2341	4123
1342	2431	4213
1324	3124	4231
1423	3142	4312
1432	3241	4321

Did you make a set? **YES!**

Basic Math Skills 3

Line Segments

Draw a line from letter to letter.

Example $\overline{XY}$ $\overline{YZ}$ $\overline{XZ}$

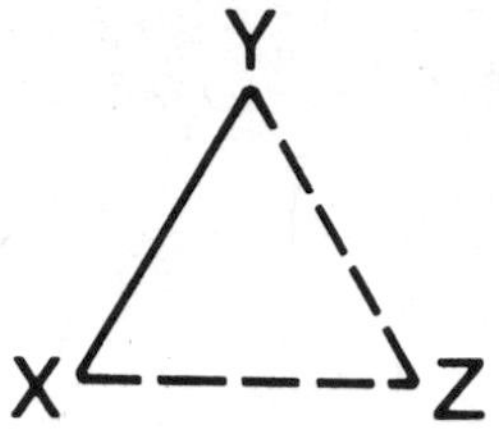

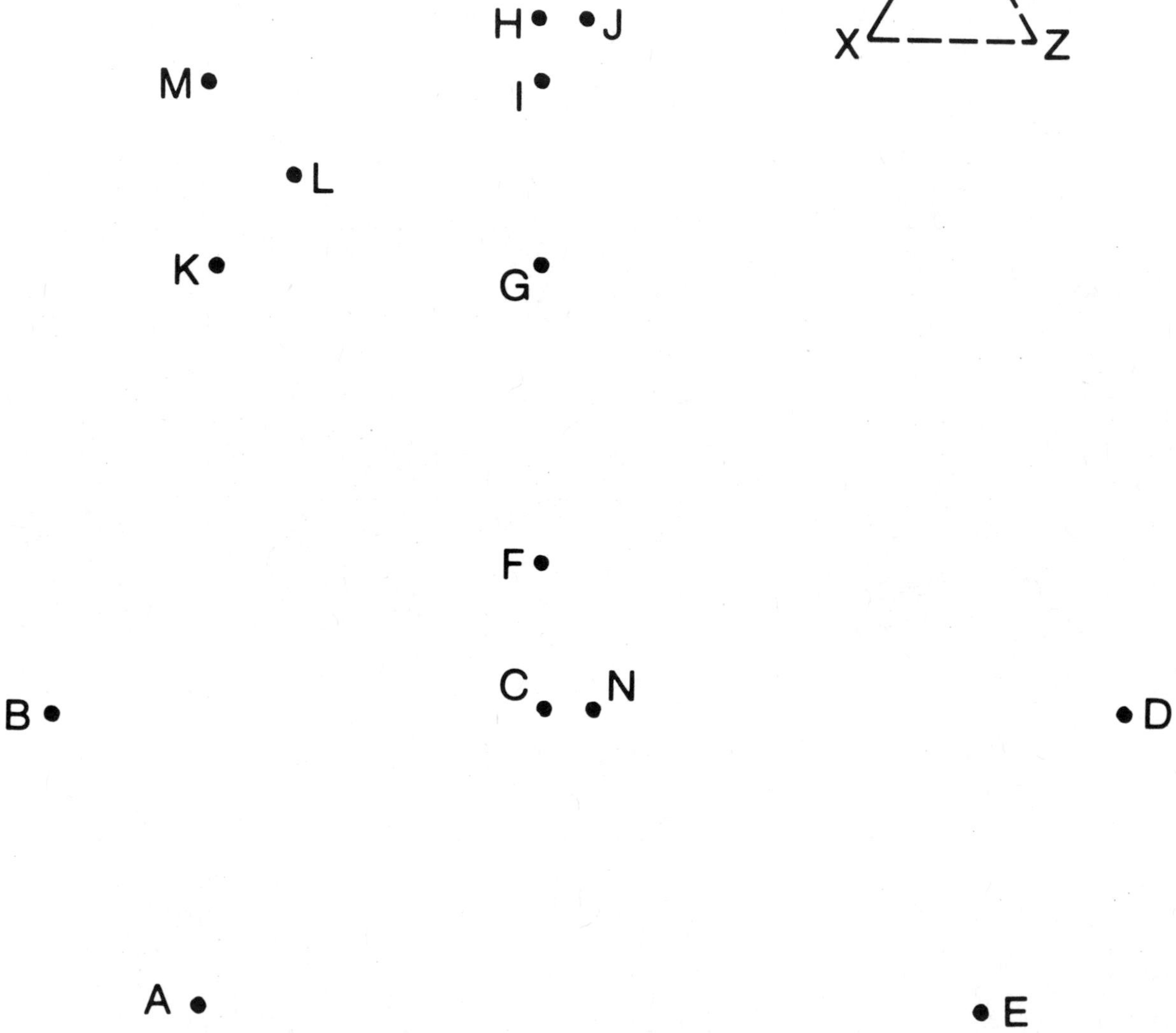

H• •J

M•

•L

K•

I•

G•

F•

C• •N

B•

•D

A •

•E

$\overline{AB}$ $\overline{EA}$ $\overline{GH}$ $\overline{LK}$ $\overline{BD}$ $\overline{GF}$ $\overline{JN}$

$\overline{IM}$ $\overline{KG}$ $\overline{DE}$ $\overline{FC}$ $\overline{ML}$ $\overline{HJ}$

This is a _____ .

Basic Math Skills 3

Line Segments

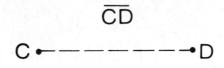

$\overline{CD}$

C •– – – – –• D

A • B •

F • G • C •

E • D •

$\overline{BG}$	$\overline{BC}$
$\overline{CG}$	$\overline{CD}$
$\overline{DG}$	$\overline{DE}$
$\overline{EG}$	$\overline{EF}$
$\overline{AG}$	$\overline{FA}$
$\overline{FG}$	$\overline{AB}$

$\overline{AB}$	$\overline{GI}$	$\overline{WY}$	$\overline{QR}$	$\overline{EF}$
$\overline{BH}$	$\overline{FZ}$	$\overline{YZ}$	$\overline{RS}$	$\overline{XY}$
$\overline{AH}$	$\overline{IJ}$	$\overline{KL}$	$\overline{ST}$	$\overline{VW}$
$\overline{BC}$	$\overline{JK}$	$\overline{ZI}$	$\overline{TU}$	$\overline{GH}$
$\overline{CD}$	$\overline{KP}$	$\overline{LM}$	$\overline{UV}$	$\overline{QV}$
$\overline{DE}$	$\overline{PQ}$	$\overline{MN}$	$\overline{WX}$	$\overline{NO}$
$\overline{OP}$				

Make 25

9	8	3	5	6	6	6	7	8
6	9	3	7	7	4	6	8	2
9	3	3	9	1	7	8	5	5
1	4	7	4	9	8	8	4	5
8	4	9	9	1	4	6	2	2
7	7	3	8	9	7	4	7	8
7	7	3	6	8	6	8	6	8
3	2	7	4	5	8	6	3	6

How many 25s did you find? ___

Line Segments

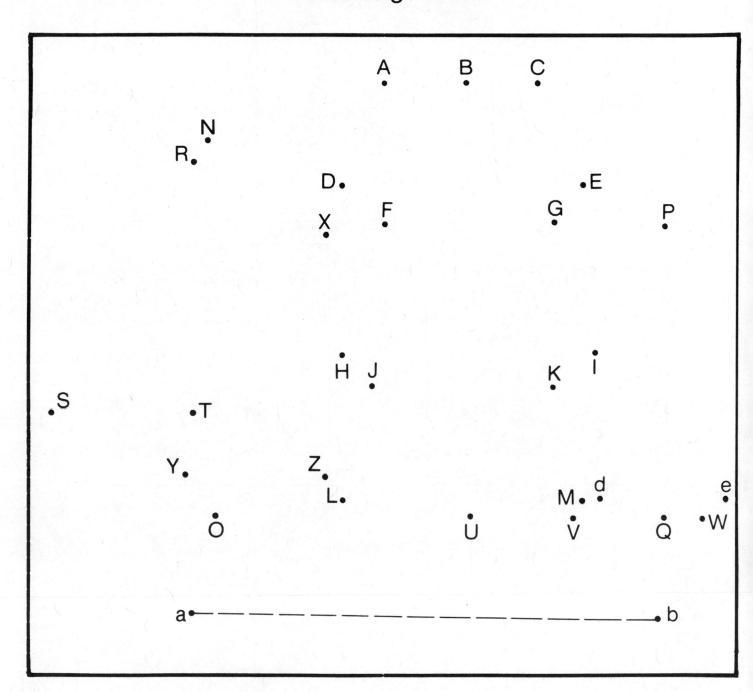

a̶b̶	$\overline{RS}$	$\overline{TR}$	$\overline{UV}$	$\overline{FH}$	$\overline{Sa}$	$\overline{Wb}$
$\overline{NO}$	$\overline{OU}$	$\overline{XZ}$	$\overline{AD}$	$\overline{JK}$	$\overline{QW}$	$\overline{LJ}$
$\overline{BU}$	$\overline{ST}$	$\overline{DE}$	$\overline{CE}$	$\overline{HI}$	$\overline{KM}$	$\overline{Pe}$
$\overline{PQ}$	$\overline{AC}$	$\overline{YZ}$	$\overline{GI}$	$\overline{FG}$	$\overline{de}$	$\overline{Pd}$
$\overline{SO}$	$\overline{XY}$	$\overline{VQ}$	$\overline{LM}$			

Basic Math Skills 3

Target Practice

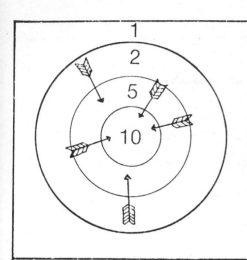

Robin Hood

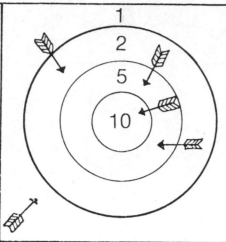

Sheriff of Nottingham

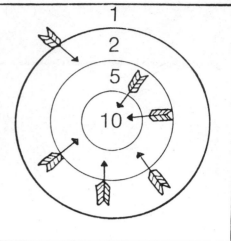

King Richard

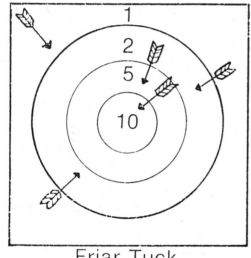

Friar Tuck

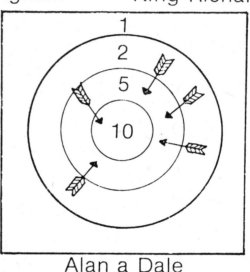

Alan a Dale

1. Total score for five arrows:
   Robin Hood _____ Alan a Dale _____
   Friar Tuck _____ King Richard _____
   Sheriff of Nottingham _____

2. Who scored the most? _____
   Who scored the least? _____

3. What is the largest possible score
   for five arrows? _____

   Show your answer here

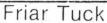

Basic Math Skills 3

Measure and draw.

(This is tricky. Be very careful!)

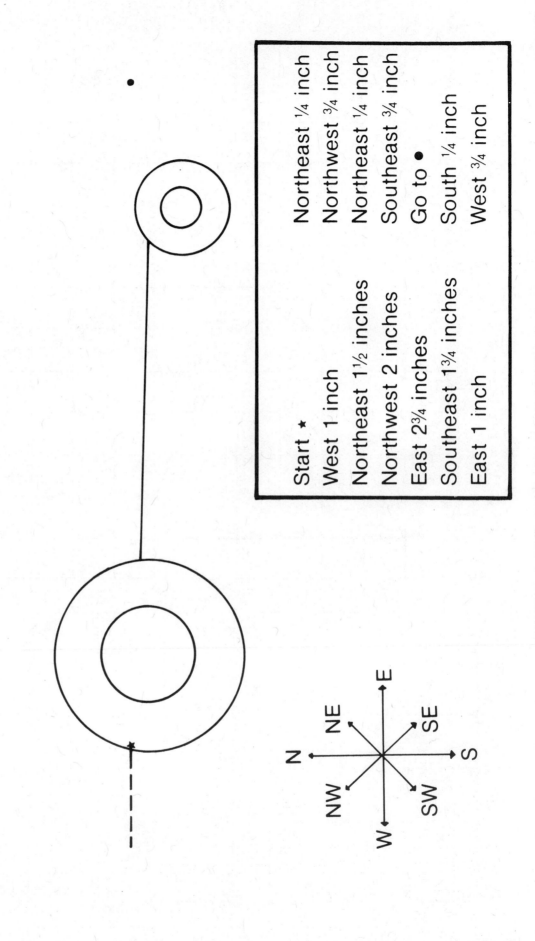

Start ★
West 1 inch
Northeast 1½ inches
Northwest 2 inches
East 2¾ inches
Southeast 1¾ inches
East 1 inch

Northeast ¼ inch
Northwest ¾ inch
Northeast ¼ inch
Southeast ¾ inch
Go to ●
South ¼ inch
West ¾ inch

Basic Math Skills 3

Find the Mystery Creature

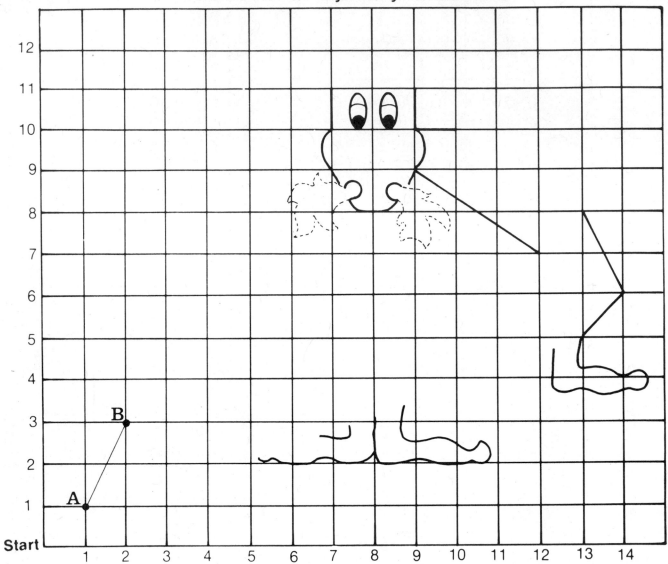

Start

over	up	write
1	1	A
2	3	B
4	4	C
7	8	D
6	5	E
8	6	F
10	7	G
13	8	H
11	8	I
11	9	J
10	9	K
10	10	L
9	11	M

over	up	write
11	11	N
10	12	O
8	12	P
7	11	Q
5	11	R
6	12	S
11	6	T
9	5	U
13	5	V
2	1	W
3	2	X
5	3	Y
7	4	Z

Draw	
A to B	H to I
B to X	I to J
X to C	J to K
C to Y	K to L
Y to E	M to N
E to Z	N to O
Z to F	O to M
F to U	M to P
U to G	P to Q
G to T	Q to S
T to H	Q to R
A to W	R to S
W to V	E to D

Basic Math Skills 3

Who am I?

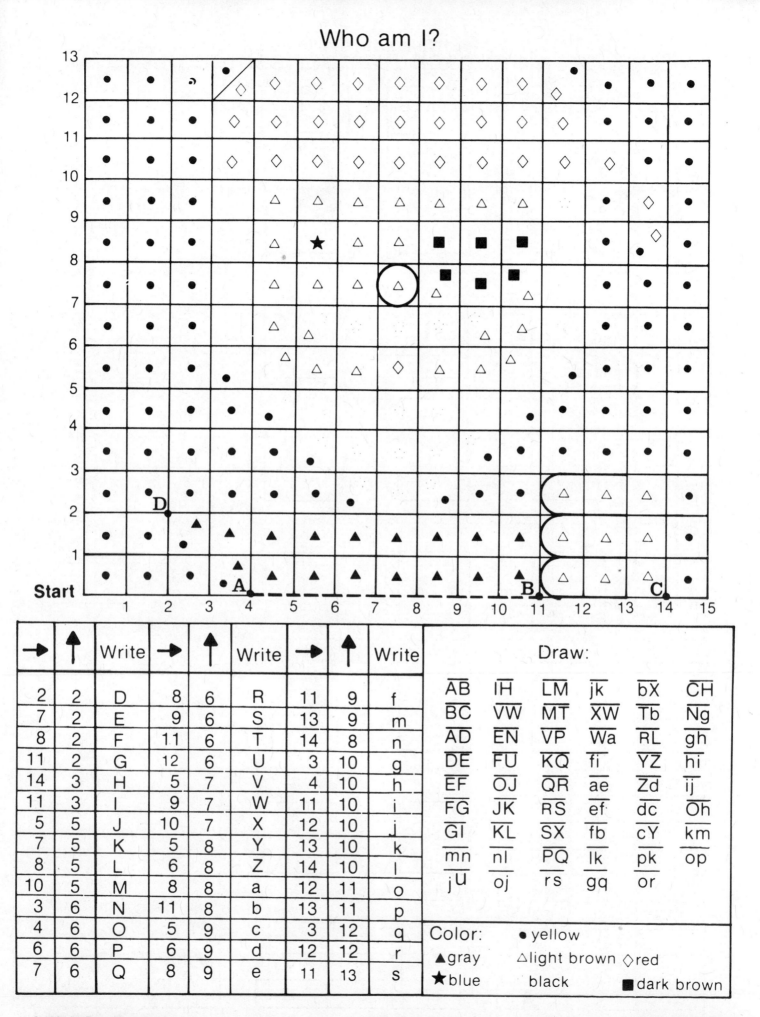

→	↑	Write	→	↑	Write	→	↑	Write
2	2	D	8	6	R	11	9	f
7	2	E	9	6	S	13	9	m
8	2	F	11	6	T	14	8	n
11	2	G	12	6	U	3	10	g
14	3	H	5	7	V	4	10	h
11	3	I	9	7	W	11	10	i
5	5	J	10	7	X	12	10	j
7	5	K	5	8	Y	13	10	k
8	5	L	6	8	Z	14	10	l
10	5	M	8	8	a	12	11	o
3	6	N	11	8	b	13	11	p
4	6	O	5	9	c	3	12	q
6	6	P	6	9	d	12	12	r
7	6	Q	8	9	e	11	13	s

Draw:

$\overline{AB}$	$\overline{IH}$	$\overline{LM}$	$\overline{jk}$	$\overline{bX}$	$\overline{CH}$
$\overline{BC}$	$\overline{VW}$	$\overline{MT}$	$\overline{XW}$	$\overline{Tb}$	$\overline{Ng}$
$\overline{AD}$	$\overline{EN}$	$\overline{VP}$	$\overline{Wa}$	$\overline{RL}$	$\overline{gh}$
$\overline{DE}$	$\overline{FU}$	$\overline{KQ}$	$\overline{fi}$	$\overline{YZ}$	$\overline{hi}$
$\overline{EF}$	$\overline{OJ}$	$\overline{QR}$	$\overline{ae}$	$\overline{Zd}$	$\overline{ij}$
$\overline{FG}$	$\overline{JK}$	$\overline{RS}$	$\overline{ef}$	$\overline{dc}$	$\overline{Oh}$
$\overline{GI}$	$\overline{KL}$	$\overline{SX}$	$\overline{fb}$	$\overline{cY}$	$\overline{km}$
$\overline{mn}$	$\overline{nl}$	$\overline{PQ}$	$\overline{lk}$	$\overline{pk}$	$\overline{op}$
$\overline{jU}$	$\overline{oj}$	$\overline{rs}$	$\overline{gq}$	$\overline{or}$	

Color: ● yellow

▲ gray △ light brown ◇ red

★ blue ■ black ■ dark brown

Basic Math Skills 3

Complete each number sentence.
Use only ☐3☐ ☐4☐ ☐5☐ .

☐ + ☐ + ☐ = 12

☐ + ☐ − ☐ = 6

☐ + ☐ − ☐ = 4

☐ + ☐ × ☐ = 27

☐ × ☐ − ☐ = 11

☐ × ☐ + ☐ = 17

☐ × ☐ × ☐ = 60

Basic Math Skills 3

Skip Counting

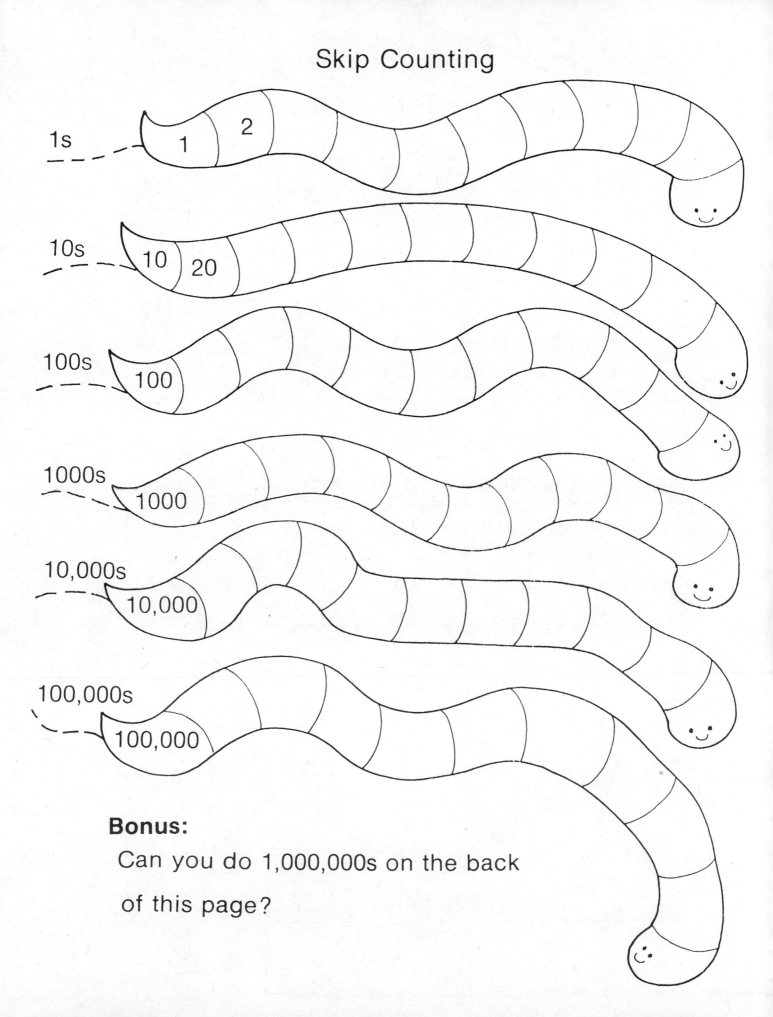

1s   1   2

10s   10   20

100s   100

1000s   1000

10,000s   10,000

100,000s   100,000

Bonus:

Can you do 1,000,000s on the back

of this page?

Basic Math Skills 3

Math Paths

 a. $1 + 2 + 3 + 4 + 5 =$ ☐

 b. $18 - 9 - 3 - 1 - 0 =$ ☐

 c. $1 \times 1 \times 2 \times 2 \times 5 =$ ☐

 d. $13 + 2 - 9 \times 2 + 4 - 3 =$ ☐

 e. $3 \times 3 - 3 + 3 \times 3 =$ ☐

 f. $16 - 8 + 0 - 6 \times 2 =$ ☐

Basic Math Skills 3

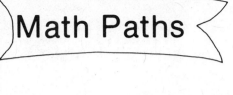

Math Paths

a. 60 − 20 + 30 + 50 − 40 = ☐

b. 46 + 24 − 24 + 12 = ☐

c. 58 + 27 − 36 + 43 − 43 = ☐

d. 370 + 158 − 101 − 158 + 122 = ☐

e. 266 − 234 + 55 + 63 − 58 = ☐

Basic Math Skills 3

What do you get if you pour boiling water down a rabbit hole?

A = 1,090,189
B = 6,420,403
C = 9,999,999
H = 2,432,107
N = 4,376,909

O = 1,777,777
R = 1,392,494
S = 4,988,740
T = 8,980,028
U = 1,935,263
Y = 1,000,000

5,387,009 −4,296,820	

7,000,000 −4,567,893	7,975,240 −6,197,463	4,286,300 +4,693,728

7,396,587 +2,603,412	6,196,247 −4,803,753	1,479,398 + 298,379	6,698,327 −1,709,587	2,494,370 +2,494,370

3,792,864 +2,627,539	8,770,359 −6,835,096	9,070,518 −4,693,609	2,288,925 +2,087,984	196,247 +803,753

Basic Math Skills 3

Magic Square

Fill in the missing numbers to equal 34 in *every* direction.

			7
	15	6	9
		3	
11	8		2

Use only these numbers.
Cross out as you go along.

1   ~~2~~   ~~3~~   4   5   ~~6~~   ~~7~~   ~~8~~

~~9~~   10   ~~11~~   12   13   14   ~~15~~   16

Basic Math Skills 3

Math Mysteries

Make three whole pizzas from the slices at the bottom of this page.
Arrange all the pizza pieces before you paste them down.

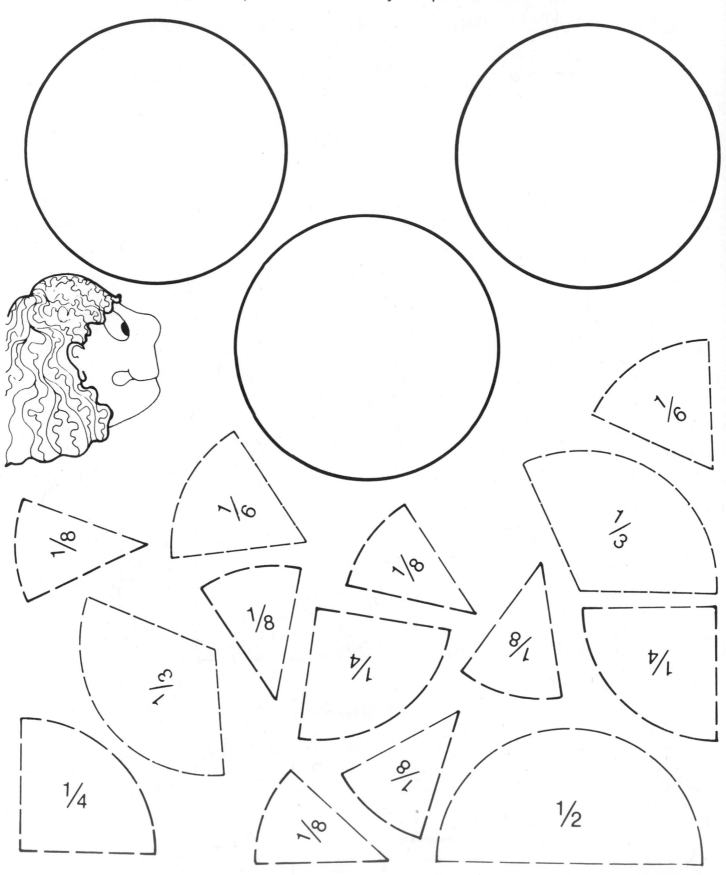

Basic Math Skills 3

Find the Mystery Number

a. George's age

       +9

       ×2

       −4

       ÷2

   −George's age

mystery number

b. your age

       +9

       ×2

       −4

       ÷2

   −your age

mystery number

c. a friend's age

       +9

       ×2

       −4

       ÷2

   −friend's age

mystery number

d. your dad's age

       +9

       ×2

       −4

       ÷2

   −dad's age

mystery number

Basic Math Skills 3

Number Challenge

How many numbers can you make using only

2 4 1 3

2413		
4132		

Did you make all 24? _____

       Basic Math Skills 3